W9-BLR-399

2/1/81

By the same author

Report from a Chinese Village
Chinese Journey
Confessions of a Disloyal European
Angkor: An Essay on Art and Imperialism
China: The Revolution Continued
Gates to Asia

China
Notebook

China Notebook

1975 - 1978

Jan Myrdal

Photographs by Gun Kessle
Translated from the Swedish by Rolf vom Dorp

Liberator Press, Chicago

Cover photo by Ray Devens

Second Printing: October 1979

Copyright © 1979 by Liberator Press

All rights reserved.
No part of this publication may be reproduced or
transmitted in any form or by any means, electronic or
mechanical, including any information storage and re-
trieval system, without the prior permission of the
publisher.

Originally published in Swedish as *Kinesiska Fragor* and
Kina Efter Mao, © Jan Myrdal 1975, 1977, by AB P A
Norstedt & Soners Förlag, Stockholm, and Ordfronts
Förlag, Stockholm, Sweden.

Library of Congress Catalog Card Number 79-88412

ISBN 0-930720-58-X (paper)
       0-930720-59-8 (cloth)

Manufactured in the United States of America

Contents

1978

A View from Peking

Coming up to Peking this autumn of 1978 after shooting documentary films on the struggle for the four modernizations in the cities and countryside of China, I reread these notes before their publication in English.

The last four years have been momentous ones in China. These notes, which cover this period, were written as articles for different newspapers and magazines. Most of the articles were written for *Expressen* (*The Express*) of Stockholm, a liberal evening paper with a circulation of 500,000. Some were written for *Svenska Dagbladet* (*The Swedish Daily*) of Stockholm, the leading conservative paper in Sweden. Other articles were written for *Folket i Bild/Kulturfront* (*The People in Pictures/Cultural Front*), a progressive biweekly (somewhat like the French *Regards* of the thirties) with a circulation of 40,000.

Several of the articles were written at an hour's notice and telephoned from Tsingtao to Stockholm in order to reach that city in time for the early afternoon edition. The articles both reflect China and the view I then had and could have had of Chinese developments.

This is an important point. After all, some of these notes that are now being published were written four years ago. I still find them valid. They reflect the way things looked at the time.

Of course these notes are a selection. If I republished every word I wrote for the press during these years it would make a far thicker volume. But I have selected the following articles so as to give both a picture of the time when they were written and a better understanding of what is happening today.

There is a speculative and metaphysical trend of writing on China that is close to theology. Pekingologists of Hong Kong or strange breeds of university leftists in Europe and the United States deduce reality from documents and theory.

But China is so much simpler. Common folk struggle for a better life. This struggle is a real struggle. It is far easier for a Minnesota farmer to understand the Chinese realities than it is for a highly trained European specialist in Eastern Languages and Pekingology to get a grip on the real contradictions and conflicts in China.

I am not writing this out of an anti-intellectual bias. I am an intellectual and am interested in theory. I am quite prepared to write on the structure of Balzacian realism or of the first attempt to rationalize racism in eighteenth century France and, in fact, do write such works. But the real-life struggles in China are not the reflections of theoretical disputes in Peking. In China, as in Sweden or the United States, the concrete struggles are the determining factor.

Professor Bettelheim is disenchanted by developments in China.* He considers them to represent a counter-revolution. But when asked to go to China and investigate the situation for himself, he refuses. He does not want to let the incidental reality interfere with his theoretical studies. He is a metaphysician!

There are simple truths about political and social reality that every working man in China, Sweden or the United States understands but that are like a closed book to the metaphysical intellectuals. This is the case whether they be honest working professors like Bettelheim or like those university leftists who one year reach their revolutionary happiness through what they believe to be Mao Tsetung Thought and the next year expand their inner consciousness through yoga and breathing exercises.

The fact that Chinese developments have been distorted through reporting that is often metaphysical, when not downright hostile, is also an expression of the political and social struggles in China these last ten years or so.

Many groups and small parties that called themselves Marxist-Leninist in Europe were disrupted and more or less smashed in the late sixties and early seventies. This was partly

* Charles Bettelheim, a French economist, has written a number of studies about the construction of socialism in the USSR and China. In May 1977, he resigned his position as president of the Franco-Chinese Friendship Association in opposition to China's present course of development.

due to the maneuvers of the ultra-left in China, who sent letters and advice to their followers abroad. This continued during the seventies through the "gang of four."* As yet this question has not been fully clarified even in China. But it had a very bad effect and led to serious misunderstandings of Chinese realities. And, of course, to disaster for the groups concerned in the different countries outside China.

There is no lack of material on China, though much of it is of a rather special kind, internal state and Party documents. Some are published officially and some leaked to Hong Kong, where they sometimes have been published as is and sometimes in tampered form. Especially during the time when the "gang of four" controlled mass media and propaganda, these documents were frothy and vague and full of rhetoric. Even today the class struggle, the struggle between two lines, continues in China and is reflected in the writings There are persons in key positions who want to sabotage the four modernizations. They are still planting documents and articles in the Hong Kong press, documents of doubtful authenticity.

The ever more open debate and discussion in China is correcting this situation. When people speak out and write their opinions plainly on the wall posters for everyone to see and discuss, facts get sorted out from fiction and right and wrong get clarified.

But still the mass of material on China of a very special kind makes it possible for both "left" and right Pekingologists to indulge in metaphysical discussions. A large part of these notes was written as open or hidden polemics against this metaphysical trend.

---

* The "gang of four" were all members of the Central Committee of the Chinese Communist Party. They were removed from office after the death of Mao Tsetung, when they plotted to seize state power and restore capitalism in China.

Chiang Ching, Chairman Mao's wife, was head of the gang. Other members were: Chang Chun-Chiao, Yao Wen-yuan and Wang Hung-wen. In the years preceding their overthrow, the gang sabotaged the national economy and had an especially pernicious influence in cultural spheres and in propaganda work.

Reading through the 1975 articles for *The Express* from Liu Lin after now staying there and working on a film about the brigade, I see what has changed. But I also see the basic problems that remain.

In 1977 the brigade wrote me. They had received and discussed my articles. The poor and lower-middle peasants had gone through what I had written on the brigade. They had found the articles interesting and true, they wrote. When I came back to the brigade in 1978 and stayed for some time, people said that the articles in the main were correct.

I met some of the people who had been young Red Guards [rebel groups which arose at schools and universities during the Cultural Revolution—ed.] in 1969 and whom I at that time had interviewed. They had a copy of *China: The Revolution Continued.** We discussed the book. They said that it reflected what they themselves had seen and understood at that time. And they did not deny the experiences of their own lives: "The long marches were the happiest times in my life," said one woman who had long since married, settled and had children.

The cadre who had mismanaged funds was back. He sat at the conference table during the meeting of the brigade committee, and nobody mentioned what had been done. If I had not known of his past, no one would have discussed it with me. "He has made self-criticism. He has turned a new leaf. It is not forgotten but nobody should speak of it. He is a good communist again now."

The struggle against those trying to "go through the back door" is even sharper in China now than in 1975. In a situation where rules and regulations had been to a large degree abolished, many had tried to use pull, the influence of parents or relatives, to get favors. Especially when the "gang of four" held a certain amount of power, some people could come in through the back door and climb rapidly.

Other problems remain and are being brought out in the open. Those young intellectuals who cannot study at the

* Jan Myrdal and Gun Kessle, *China: The Revolution Continued* (New York: Vintage, 1972).

universities in the big cities or who do not get posts in the big cities are not all content with working in the countryside. As far as I can see, there will be some rather sharp struggles ahead with groups that try to hang on in Shanghai or Peking without a proper job. Even if they are a small fraction of their generation, they will constitute a problem.

The articles written at the passing away of Chairman Mao and the fall of the gang reflect the situation as I saw it from Tsingtao. We spent seven months traveling through China and had come down over land by the old Silk Road, all the way from the Soviet border to Lanchow, where we had taken the train to Chengtu in Szechuan, and on to Chungking and, from there, continued down the river by boat. But Gun Kessle got ill along the road, a relapse of her old TB. We then stayed at the sanatorium of Tsingtao on the Shantung coast. There she rested and we worked on our book about the Silk Road.*

In Tsingtao Gun Kessle and I could witness the deep mourning when Chairman Mao passed away amid the great change as the "gang of four" fell. But if the change was great, it was still no change in the general line of development in China.

In Sinkiang and Kansu we had been talking with leaders of production brigades and local leading cadres and workers at the time when the influence of the "gang of four" was at its height, the summer of 1976. They were all discussing the realities of production and revolution. They were often in a bitter fight for this correct line against ultra-leftists, as in Khotan, but they kept up their efforts to increase production according to the decisions of the Fourth National People's Congress and the Conference on Learning from Tachai in Agriculture of 1975. These were the goals they talked about and struggled for that summer.

The general line of the Party did not change when the "gang of four" fell. Chairman Hua then represented the unbroken and continuous policy that the overwhelming majority of

---

* Jan Myrdal and Gun Kessle, *The Silk Road: A Journey from the High Pamirs and I-li through Sinkiang and Kansu* (New York: Pantheon, 1979).

Party cadres and masses had followed all through the years. To them there was no question that Chairman Hua would continue the policy of Chairman Mao and Premier Chou En-lai.

At that time some people were saying that the seventeen years prior to the Cultural Revolution were wasted, that they represented a black line. This was not true at that time and not true today. I met certain such people at that time and I did not believe them. They did not represent either the Party or the government. They were not to be found among the cadres working and struggling all over China to implement the decisions of the Fourth National People's Congress and the Conference on Learning from Tachai that summer of 1976 when, as we now know, the "gang of four" were making their bid for power.

Today one may meet some people in China who say that the ten years of the Cultural Revolution were wasted. That is not correct either. During the ten years from 1966 to 1976, China continued to develop. Small repair shops grew to factories, production brigades increased their yield. There were difficulties, there were also ultra-left deviations. There were bad tendencies in the Cultural Revolution as Mao Tsetung pointed out. And during the sharp struggles of 1974 and 1976, there was quite some loss to the development of China's economy. But it is as wrong to say that these ten years were wasted and represented a black line as it is to say that the seventeen years between Liberation and the Cultural Revolution were wasted and represented a black line. There have been struggles in China. There are struggles at this very moment; there will be struggles. These struggles may take different forms. But during the thirty years since Liberation, or the nearly forty-five years since Mao Tsetung and Chou En-lai became responsible for the Party line in 1935, the general line of development has remained unchanged.

Many people wonder about Teng Hsiao-ping. He was a responsible and leading cadre. He was severely criticized. He came back. He was once more criticized. He again came back as a responsible cadre and became the spokesman for China. Yes, there has been a political struggle around him. He has been criticized for mistakes and some of that criticism was correct, and he made self-criticism. In another regard, the criticism against Teng Hsiao-ping was an expression of the struggle between the two lines. He stood against the metaphysical and elitist trend of the "gang of four." One could say that the greatest mistake he committed was to slip for a moment and let the gang get a grip on him as Premier Chou En-lai was dying and Chairman Mao Tsetung was nearing death. He was not supple enough at that stage. He was too frank. That is a criticism I heard from Chinese friends.

The fact that a political leader is criticized and disappears from the first rank for some time and then once more gets a mandate to lead should not surprise us. We will be surprised only if we believe that such leaders are holy saints or born geniuses. That, of course, would be the acceptance of a *Führer* principle!

Of course there have been struggles in China. But the "gang of four" never had decisive power. The only position the gang really controlled was that of the mass media and the arts, and that is, after all, not the key position. But for all those people in Peking and abroad to whom secret documents appear to be the true reality (the greater the secrecy, the truer), the change as the "gang of four" fell was enormous.

The gang's members did much damage in the cultural field. They managed to create disorder in certain industries. But when they made a bid for power, they were smashed, not just by some leaders in Peking but by the millions and millions of Party workers supported by the masses in their hundreds of millions. The masses reacted against the "gang of four" because they saw all they had worked and sweated and struggled for during long and difficult years being threatened by loud-mouthed careerists. It's as simple as that. That made the change go calmly. There was no mass support for the "gang of four" and without mass support there can be no ruling left.

Any group that lords it over the people and subjects the masses to dictatorship, even if they say they do it for the sake of the people, is reactionary. This is so whether the group calls itself communist, democratic or revolutionary. The people are the motive force in history. There is no dictatorship of the proletariat that can be a dictatorship over the proletariat by some few. In that case it is not a dictatorship of the proletariat but a fascist dictatorship, as in the Soviet Union.

There can be no real left against the masses. Only a phony "left." That is the main point. Chiang Ching and her followers had strange habits. People did not like the way they behaved. But that is secondary. If they had in the main been doing good and correct work, people would have overlooked their peculiar habits and the rashness of Chiang Ching and might even have forgiven her personal cruelty to old acquaintances. People are broadminded. After all, she was once married to Chairman Mao Tsetung and, if a toad sits on a piece of precious jade, it is difficult to strike the toad without hurting the jade, as it has been put. But when Chiang Ching made a bid for power and really threatened China and the Chinese people's revolution, she was smashed.

Today I would write another book. The films I and Rune Hassner are working with are different.* One does not bathe twice in the same river or visit the same China twice. But these notes remain valid as written.

Jan Myrdal
Peking 1978

* Rune Hassner is a photographer and worked with Myrdal in 1978 on six films about China for Swedish television.

1975

A Chinese Village Revisited

Daycare Centers in Liu Lin

What is happening in China is very remarkable though not especially odd. China is moving forward. It is a simple truth. She is rising out of poverty and need. Not too long ago Shanghai was as inhumanly repulsive as Calcutta.

But the fact that China is moving forward strikes us forcefully because she is doing it by her own efforts. She has thus become an example. Month after month there is a growing number of government delegations and specialist groups from the third world making study trips to China.

But the way in which China is progressing and the discussions which are now taking place there are neither incomprehensible nor especially odd. In Liu Lin's production brigade, they have just recently been able to set up permanent daycare centers for the work team's children. Before this, daycare centers were only available during the rush periods of the year. Now, they are open the year round.

The children were almost as charming and trusting, and were almost as self-confident in front of adults and strangers, as were the children in daycare centers in Shanghai or Peking. Almost, but not completely, for Liu Lin lies deep in the heart of China, and daycare centers are still quite new.

The issue of daycare centers had been discussed for a long time and in depth. Theoretical debates on daycare centers and their significance had taken place before. These discussions had been pushed for by the younger women, especially by those who had been active Red Guards during the Great Proletarian Cultural Revolution. They had discussed the issue politically and had linked it to the widespread women's debates seven years back when the women enlisted support for the policy decision that men should have equal responsibility for childcare.

At that time, it had involved such things as the real (and not just theoretical) right of women to attend meetings during the evenings, to participate in discussions, and to take part in making decisions. Many men contended that they did not have breasts and that small children always cried for mama. Thus, there were biological reasons compelling them to attend the meetings and women to stay at home. Through long debates, they became convinced, theoretically at least, that their position was objectively incorrect.

Daycare centers were necessary for many reasons. The children needed them. It was a question of how the new generation would be brought up. It was important to prepare the children for the collective work now that all went to school. Otherwise, even greater differences would develop between children from the city and children from the countryside. It was indeed a difference which had to be diminished.

The daycare centers were also necessary because they freed labor power for the work teams. But this was not just important to the brigade's economic development, it would also create the preconditions for real equality between the sexes.

As long as the woman had to shoulder most of the work of the home and children and the man worked outside in production, there could not be real equality between sexes. Such a situation constantly gave birth to prejudices against women among the men. And those women who broke out of the pattern and participated in the political life as well as in the productive work often had to work double: partly at home, partly in the community.

In Liu Lin, the discussion had gone on for a long time. Those active in work among women had taken it up in 1962. And in 1969, to help liberate the women, they had won support for building an electric mill, as well as collective sewing rooms.

The great theoretical campaigns in China, for instance the campaign against Lin Piao and Confucius, have never really been abstract. The question of whether certain people are born geniuses and therefore understand everything better than others, whether such geniuses should lead and others should content themselves to listen and follow—this is not an abstract question. It really concerns each of us, in our own countries as well as in China. It is easier for us to discuss and decide on a matter once we try to rid ourselves of the notion of geniuses and elites and we instead assume responsibility for our own decisions.

And as far as women are concerned, it has always been said that they were intended for nothing other than looking after the home. And, therefore, they should always agree with those who understand the major issues better. It has also been said that they should not only respect their elders, but also obey them. And all of this, said day after day for thousands of years, leaves an impression in the back of our minds.

It is not just that people are oppressed; they are also given thoughts and notions about their own worthlessness and inferiority which oppress them. To settle accounts with that inner oppression is important. This contributes to the liberation of an enormous creative force, rich initiative and the capacity to work together for a common goal. For thousands of years, these qualities had been suppressed by longstanding prejudices about inferiority, obedience, geniuses and the people's backwardness.

If one views these campaigns from the watch towers of the Pekingologists and China-watchers, they become obscure and strange, ingeniously distorted. But if one looks at them from below, they become simple and clearly necessary. And if one does an experiment, substituting other personages for Lin Piao and Confucius, and if one looks at what is really happening in Bridgeport or Kansas, then it is not too difficult to realize that notions about geniuses and the people's ignorance and about women's peculiarity, ideas which keep mankind shackled, exist much closer to home than in China.

The feet of girls in Liu Lin were once bound so tightly that as adults they became cripples who could only stump forward. That custom was eliminated. It was not too difficult. That kind of liberation was easy to carry out once the old society had been overthrown. But liberating oneself from stunting notions takes a longer time and does not occur automatically. It is not accomplished in a day or through one discussion.

After discussions about equality seven years before, the

men in Liu Lin had said that they had been convinced in theory
that it was not necessary to have breasts to care for children.
This did not, however, mean that in practice they shared the
work of home and child rearing. But those debates
made some impression. All the work teams have now been
able to introduce daycare centers, which provide the practical
opportunity for women's liberation and equality.

The six years which had passed since I last was in Liu Lin
had indeed brought big improvements. The new school had
been finished. The teachers had taken over the old school and
transformed it into residences for the teachers. They had built
250 "stone grottoes," which really are not grottoes, but a kind
of house of stone with barrel-arched construction. They are
cool in summer and warm in winter. Almost every family has
now procured the "four bigs" (bicycle, radio, sewing machine,
and wristwatch). There were thus adequate material resources
to set up with one's own means daycare centers in the brigade
through self-reliance.

But the decision on daycare centers was not the same as the
realization of this decision. Eighteen-year-old Chang Ai-liang
took care of the sixth work team's daycare center. She was
from Yenan, where her father was a sanitation worker. She had
left the lower middle-school and moved to Liu Lin. It had not
been too easy to get the daycare center started. It had been
difficult to get the money to cover everything.

Consequently, the daycare centers were much too shabby in
the beginning, and many parents had not wanted to send their
children there. But gradually the kinks were worked out and
the daycare centers are pretty good now.

But there were other difficulties. Many parents, especially
women, had said that daycare centers could be a good thing
and that they had talked about this for many years but that
their children did not need daycare centers. Other people's
children, perhaps, needed the daycare centers.

Some said right out that it was only the youth who spoke
out for daycare centers, but the youth, clearly, did not have any
children of their own. A few women also said that these girls

who spoke so much about caring for the children and who would care for the children of others had not born any of their own children and did not have any real experience. "How could they then say that they know how to take care of children?" they had asked. They did not believe in the collective rearing of children.

There were also many children who came one day and then never showed up again. They felt that the daycare center was unpleasant. They thought it was more fun to be at home. There were also a few children who had cried and fought. Indeed, in the beginning it had been difficult.

But Chang Ai-liang had gone around to the parents and talked about it with them. She had also proven that the daycare center had received better financial support and that it was no longer so skimpily equipped. Chang Ai-liang had shown that she really could take care of the children and she had discussed all the aspects of the daycare work with the parents. Members of the youth organization had also gone around and spoken with the parents.

She had shown the parents that good results came from the efforts at the children's daycare centers and that she truly cared for the children. So now, all families send their children to the daycare center and say that the collective rearing of children is a good thing. Taking care of the children was not so easy. Especially since the children themselves were not accustomed to such things as the center, and they felt it was unpleasant or they wanted to fight.

But she had talked to others and asked advice, learning from the experiences of other daycare centers. She then began with small games and infant gymnastics, taught songs, and told about the People's Liberation Army.

Once a week, she took her own money and bought a few sweets for the children. She was gradually able to introduce more serious things into the activities. The children went together to the fields to participate in collective work. And she took them to old cadres, to men and women who were able to recount how life had been before and how they had lived, worked and fought. So now there were both games and seriousness. Now the children also wanted to be in the collective.

Liu Lin's production brigade is not a shining model of a brigade in China. It lies just outside of Yenan and does not belong to the most successful of brigades in the area.

That daycare centers had been set up in its work teams, and that the children now like to go to the centers and play singing games and visit the homes of the elderly and ask them how it was before, and that the young girl who cares for the daycare centers speaks of them as a step in the struggle for real women's equality, and that it is a matter of fighting the cult of geniuses and notions of people's ignorance and old notions of the inferiority of women—nothing of this is odd. It is, however, very remarkable.

The Express
7/27/75

On Equality

On the evening of July 2, 1975, the members of the fifth work team of the Liu Lin production brigade are sitting around after the end of a long work day and discussing the question of bourgeois right under socialism until late that night.

Such discussions are taking place throughout China. This is a fact. But it is important to go a step back to get a general view, to be able to see the context, and to understand what it really is they are discussing.

Six years ago (1969), the thorough political discussions during the Cultural Revolution had lead to a series of concrete decisions in Liu Lin. The brigade's organization had been simplified and democratized.

The economic policies of the brigade had been altered. Its members were to concentrate on construction work and on investment. They were to build up the reserve of grain, develop the preventive health services and the collective medical services. They were to concentrate on schools and daycare centers and see to it that the basic housing standards of the members were raised. The resources were to be used primarily to increase production and to finance different collective measures.

Now the results of these policies had become clear. Liu Lin had seen some significant changes. The brigade had been mechanized. What had once been a little back alley corner for bicycle repairs had now become a complete plant, which was making the leap from a repair shop to a small-scale industry.

Brigade members themselves could already manufacture the new sprinkler system; the parts were cast and reworked according to drawings obtained in the capital of the province.

The machine assembly area was expanding. A worker, who six years ago as a young fellow had liked to lend a hand at bicycle repairs, had become a craftsman and was responsible for the brigade's new and expensive machines.

The brigade now had two trucks and three tractors and had even obtained a Caterpillar tractor for installation work up in the valley. After extensive and intensive discussion, the members had finally decided not only to terrace the hills but also to concentrate on new techniques and shape large fields suited to rational large-scale production and able to accommodate tractors.

This had been one of the decisive political discussions of the past years, and the issue had not been decided in a jiffy. But they had finally been able to unite around heavy emphasis on a major project. This was even more necessary, as the railroad was now being laid from Yenan and the railroad bed would occupy a section of the field down in the valley towards Ten-Mile Village.

During the spring, the brigade had thus been able to discuss and fix its first real long-term plan, covering the period up to 1980. It anticipated a heavy increase in grain production, as well as fruit and vegetable cultivation. That fixed plan was, said Feng Chang-yeh, a contribution to socialist construction.

For twenty years, Feng Chang-yeh had been in leadership. First in the higher-level agricultural producers' cooperative, and later, after the setting up of the people's commune, in the production brigade. During these years, great changes had been wrought, and Feng Chang-yeh as well as others had been criticized. But he had been re-elected. Now, he had become "Old Fang" or "Old Secretary."

Feng Chang-yeh felt that they should indeed not underestimate what had been done, but, at the same time, they should view the situation realistically. There were serious shortcomings and major difficulties. The fact that returns were less than they should and could be did not only come from unfavorable external conditions which could easily be changed. They were also caused by an insufficiently high level of consciousness among the people. He could agree that since 1962 there had been very big developments in the Liu Lin production brigade. But if brigade members looked forward, not backward, then they could understand that much remained undone.

China's economy is developing, and the country is progressing. But the prudence in judgment which Feng showed and which is not some false humility, but a clear and uncliched description of the real situation, is now very typical for China. The progress there has been so great and so visible that they need not pretend it is greater than it really is.

It is not true that progress is simply in the realm of economics, that progress is for the sake of statistics. The people of Liu Lin had built new schools and set up daycare centers, and health services had been improved. In 1969, Wang You-nan had been the only health service worker; now there were eight co-workers in the work brigade. They could handle most of the cases in the brigade, and only the most serious cases had to be treated in Yenan. The main emphasis was still the work of improving hygiene and of preventative measures against illness.

During winter and spring, mainly colds and respiratory infections and, during summer, stomach infections made people sick. By organizing the work in health service for these eventualities, they were able to reduce illness in the brigade from 3,000 cases in 1970 to a little over 1,000 cases in 1974.

The members had received new homes and the brigade had just been able to change to collective financing of home construction. This was a great step forward. (They paid one yuan per year for the right to use these dwellings.) The standard of living climbed, needs increased and the supply of goods multiplied not only in the department stores of large cities, but also in the stores of Yenan and Ten-Mile Village. In spring, Liu Lin's production brigade also opened a new store for consumer goods in the middle of the main village.

The purpose of the economic policies in China has always been one expressed by Mao's words "serve the people." The discussion has never been between those who want people "to have it good" and those who want people "to do without." The great debates about investments and emphasis on installation work in Liu Lin seven or eight years back had led to the decisions which brought about schools and health services as well as new homes and, for that matter, private bicycles.

Under this kind of situation, a new nationwide discussion was initiated in China. One which in its own way was as pervasive as the great discussions during the Cultural Revolution. It was Mao Tsetung who initiated it; and he took up the issues which are at the core of these policies. What's really happening with equality under socialism?

For sure, it is a theoretical question. Marx wrote about it, as did Lenin. For this reason, the question of what equality means under socialism is not an abstract one. It is indeed so that there is not, nor can there be, equality under socialism. Under it, everyone is paid according to work and not need. China is a socialist country, a socialistically-developing country of the third world, and it may well be a long time before China's economy makes it materially possible to satisfy all the needs of its citizens. So, for a long time to come, inequality will remain. This is a dangerous and very serious situation. For under these circumstances, individuals and groups are born every day who see themselves receiving material advantages from this shortage of equality, and who therefore will seek to safeguard them, who will make them into privileges.

We can see how in the Soviet Union such privileged groups gradually formed a new class and ultimately set up a new class rule, based on total control over the means of production and protected by a strongly expanded police force.

This is why the fifth work team in Liu Lin's production brigade is staying up until late at night on July 2, discussing bourgeois right under socialism. Li Hai-tsai makes an introductory speech. It is a very fine review of the questions of commodity and small-scale production, and of how capitalism is constantly reborn here in the countryside. Li Hai-tsai quotes Marx, Lenin and Mao Tsetung, but he makes it very personal.

It has been a long work day. First one, and then another brigade member blinks his tired eyes. Li Hai-tsai has been politically active as long as I have known him; but they hardly ever talked at this political level in Liu Lin in 1969, and not at all in 1962. This is of great significance. The most serious questions, those which concern the future of all the people, are no longer discussed in closed offices, but among and by the people. It is not said that people "do not understand theory and complex ideas."

Theory is not really so difficult either. How does it look in Liu Lin and what kind of inequality hides behind equality? Two families surnamed Chen are sitting here. Both have three in the family who work. Both earn equally as much. This is equal. But the one family Chen also has three non-working members and this is not equal. Thus, this family Chen does not live as well as the first. Is it correct that there should be such differences?

And how are work points really set? How is it that the work day for women gives fewer points? Why should physical strength give extra points? And the youth are not contented. The older people have awarded themselves full points and given the youth fewer points, but then they let the youth do all the heavy work. "The heaviest work should be for the one receiving the most points."

But others feel that this expression shows a poor attitude toward work, reflecting low morale on the job. One does not just work for the sake of points.

Everyone discusses the matter. Certainly, it is not possible to eliminate all inequalities by giving to each according to need. There is not enough to go around. The brigade's members must continue to give to each other according to work, but they can improve basic security.

Now, besides the income from work, there is also a basic security which reaches all, even infants and people on pensions. It covers only grain; it should be expanded to cover even fruit and vegetables. There is an obstacle to providing the people with the best possible medical services. If an illness becomes too extended and costly, the revolutionary committee will have to make a special decision that the costs be covered by the collective medical services. This obstacle can be removed and the guarantee become complete.

This is the way the debate is going in the fifth work team in Liu Lin's production brigade, and so it goes in the work teams and factories and schools in all of China. . . .

The Express
7/30/75

But What About the Back Door?

Among us there are many who deep down inside themselves feel it is better to be rich, healthy and beautiful, than to be poor, worn out and stooped. Such people even crack jokes about this.

There are actually a good number of such people in China. But they do not talk loudly about it. It is far more comfortable to work on the Party's Central Committee in Peking, have a nice home, send one's children to nice daycare centers and listen to interesting political discussions in the park, than it is to be a Party member in the fifth work team in Liu Lin's production brigade, get up with the sun and toil in the fields up in the hills to get in the crops.

This is the way it is. And were it not like this, then it would really be quite easy to carry out revolutions and transform the society. And it is this simple truth which is the basis for much of the politics bearing the stamp of Mao Tsetung.

Take for instance the question of students. Now 93% of all children of school age in China attend school. It is not said that "all children" go to school. This is just not true. There has been a big struggle to set up schools for a quarter of humanity: schools on the steppe and in the desert, schools in the mountain villages and in the forests, as well as schools in the rice region or the loess region. This giant undertaking continues. Ninety-three percent says a lot more about the progress than does a general, careless "all children."

Before the Cultural Revolution, there was a strong tendency to run the schools from the center. It was said that the poor peasants could neither read nor write, and that, therefore, they should not be involved in overseeing school work. That tendency was broken during the Cultural Revolution. Now it is the poor and lower-middle peasants in Liu Lin's production brigade who have the power over the school and discuss, together with teachers and students, the curriculum, the length of semesters and the direction of school work.

There are of course central proposals and teaching aids, but it is the people in Liu Lin who have a school for their children. It is not Peking which placed a school in Liu Lin. Nor have the people in Liu Lin organized their school to churn out officials. Before, children were sent to school only to climb up the official career ladder. It is no longer like this. Not only because 93% of China's people cannot get an official career (who would feed all those officials?), but also because the whole system of officials has been done away with and the mandarin buttons have for a long time only been seen in the museum.

But, indeed, the thousand-year tradition still lives on. There are also real differences between town and country, between intellectual work and manual work, between industry and

contended that people really have no understanding for big issues but are mainly interested in how they can get hold of oil, salt, meat and fuel.

In their innermost thoughts, such cadres feel that Mao Tsetung only called for a token phrase when he sought the right to strike written into the constitution of China. For they are of the opinion that the workers really understand nothing and do not have to strike. And around these people, the official ideology is gradually transformed into the ideology of officialdom; and point by point, they divert China's course, preferably in the name of efficiency or production or the good order.

By necessity, such strata arise. In the beginning, such cadres are themselves scarcely conscious that they are in the process of changing themselves under the influence of higher social position and incipient personal privileges. When they become conscious of it, they are already deeply convinced that Mao Tsetung was wrong and all this about mass line, broad democracy and open discussion is simply a pain in the neck.

And they begin to ogle the Soviet Union where such things are not found, where status brings privileges and where power now also gives a certain security and a comfortable old age. The Soviet ambassadors do not go out into agriculture when they return home. They are awarded gold stars instead.

The great thing with China is that the Chinese people are building their country by their own efforts and are creating new conditions of human dignity. But there are many problems, and the diversity which is necessary can grow into a contradiction. A struggle between two lines is going on, and China could change colors. And instead of the mass line, by which China is now growing both with difficulty and success, a small ruling elite could spring up, like in the Soviet Union, to protect their privileges. Such an elite may by all means oppress and silence the people who feed them. What speaks against such a new class taking power is that the people of Liu Lin, as well as throughout China, know from thousand-year experience and from Mao Tsetung's remarks that it could really happen. And the people of Liu Lin are therefore striving to prevent this.

One essential part of this is that they are seeking so consciously to avail themselves of their newly-won freedom to discuss and to decide upon general issues.

The Express
8/11/75

To Put Mao Tsetung Up For Debate, Too

"Is it possible to criticize something of what Chairman Mao has said or written without the person who is doing the criticizing consequently being regarded as a reactionary?" An Associate Professor Per Sörbom [history professor in Uppsala, Sweden—ed.] wondered this recently in *The Express* of July 18, 1975.

The issue is, he wrote, a serious one and is not to be used as a trick for ensnaring one into debate.

It is a serious question. It is also an important one, and it should be discussed, without technical tricks of debate, by exactly we who harbor friendship with China. Nor is it an issue unknown to Mao Tsetung. Also for him, it is a central question of how he can succeed to have his words read and not just have them drowned out by tribute and cheers. He has touched upon this in many discussions in the past decade.

If China goes awry and a new ruling class crystallizes out of the current social struggle, then all signs point to such a new class rule transforming Mao into a picture, an idol. His words would be declared eternally valid. Mao Tsetung Thought would become a theology. His words would no longer be studied, only deciphered.

There are many historic examples of this. What happened with Marx and Lenin in Moscow could also happen with Mao Tsetung in Peking. The words and the living ideas could be transformed into dead formulas, buried in vaulted institutions and a life's work devoted to the liberation of humanity could become a legitimization for a new and corrupt class rule.

The question of whether it is possible to make Mao Tsetung's words the subject of debate is thus no technical trick in some local debate; it is a large and central question. But to reason this out, one has to see it in perspective.

Certainly there are Chinese who are clearly and directly hostile to Mao Tsetung and what he stands for. They are vociferous in Taiwan and Hong Kong and, here and there, in certain overseas Chinese groups. They are also found in China. They are the losers of the long civil war which ended with Chiang Kai-shek's defeat and flight. It is a handful, but in China such a handful perhaps includes a few million.

The hostility is rarely shown openly in China. For the only one in Liu Lin's production brigade whom I could possibly imagine harboring such a deep and principled hostility would be the son of the former landowner who was once imprisoned for counter-revolutionary activity But if ho harbois such thoughts, he is careful in disclosing them.

The reason is very simple. I am sitting and writing this in Södermanland [southwest of Stockholm, Sweden—ed.]. Once this area had a sharecropping economy. If I wanted to get into hot water, I would go out to the Berga Manor, go in the barn and tell the agricultural workers there that I am contemplating working for the restoration of sharecropping and they should now know their place. It is not, however, just a reform of the wage system which has been carried out in China, but also a real revolution. Such a principled hostility is therefore experienced as a direct threat to the very existence of the overwhelming majority. It is also treated as such.

But I do not know if there are so many who dream about such a restoration in China. I doubt it. In New York in February 1966, I participated in a TV debate. I spoke of the need for diplomatic ties between the United States and China. Afterwards, some overseas Chinese wanted to argue with me. Actually they had been opponents of the People's Republic. They had been in the KMT and had fled. It was a time in the U.S. when everything teeter-tottered. Should the war against the Vietnamese people be further escalated or would it be possible for Washington to change its course? Already at that time, however, the opponents to the People's Republic, who lost both property and power through the revolution, did not want to attack Mao Tsetung. And that unwillingness to go against him typifies even his opponents within China. Its basis is that Mao Tsetung really is a great figure in China's history.

Neither myths nor propagandistic staging are needed to make him stand out as a figure of world history. The policies for which he has been responsible have in the course of half a century shaken our world. His enemies, as well as Mao Tsetung himself, are conscious of this. Not even in the Kremlin are they unconscious of this. The old joke from the early sixties, that in future encyclopedias Khrushchev would be described as a Ukrainian art critic at the time of Mao Tsetung, is becoming less of a joke with each year.

Mao Tsetung is clearly conscious of the social power occupied by such a historic figure and has had an objective picture of himself in relationship to his historical greatness. He has therefore been politically able to make use of that power.

This is very uncommon. It is more common that historical figures are overpowered by their greatness and become the victims of it. Let me give an example.

In 1814, when Napoleon Bonaparte faced his political life's final crises and his own aristocracy was opening Paris to the allies, the people of the suburbs demanded arms. Napoleon is an historic figure and he knew it. People still saw him in the greatness of the revolution. In 1814, he held that power in his hands but was incapable of using it. As Louis Blanc said, he loved to see people in uniform but he had violent aversion to the people in blue shirts. He thus had to flee, and his political lifework crumbled before him.

In 1966, the revolution Mao Tsetung had led to victory began to show signs of getting stale. A new ruling class had begun to announce its arrival. Mao Tsetung did not have any institutional means of preventing this. He already saw himself treated as an old revered idol without real life. At that time he showed that he was prepared to make use of his historical greatness as a social force. It gave him the opportunity to take the initiative: Bombard the headquarters! This would trigger a mass struggle, unleashing enormous social forces who, in a political revolution, redirected the society on a revolutionary course and created new social structures.

The difference stems from the character of the leader. Mao Tsetung's greatness has been that he has not dreaded the blue shirts but has dared to unleash these forces. The danger is obvious, that the leader can be immobilized by praise. What may be a strength one day can become a fetter the next.

Mao Tsetung reacted very strongly when he opened the newspaper and found his own picture on every page, each tribute more exaggerated than the last. The fact that he reacted against this form of personality cult was not because of some sort of reverse vanity. He reacted against it as a harmful, socially dangerous, political phenomena. His writings were portrayed as being eternally true, while his writings themselves contended that such eternal truths could not exist. He was described as a genius who stepped out of history and who shaped events after his mind, while all his work strove to show that such geniuses did not exist and it is the people who are the driving force in history. With an ever greater tribute to his person and his words, all that thought for which he served as an interpreter was turned inside out. It was, as he himself said, to wave the red flag against the red flag.

Mao Tsetung represents the revolution's victory and China's rebirth. He represents a China which no longer is degraded but which is growing ever stronger, and a life which is getting better each day. The comparison between the dark and evil past and today's tremendous progress in each village, in every city, and at every workplace in China gives a complete, unequivocal picture. This is why his prestige is so enormous, a prestige which is based upon concrete conditions. This is why those who have become his opponents have not appeared as his opponents but as his "best pupils."

Lin Piao sought personal power and success and the opportunity to pursue his own policies. He did this by bringing himself as close as possible to Mao Tsetung, by presenting himself as his most loyal apprentice, by never opening his mouth without quoting Mao Tsetung. Above the table, he lied and spoke cordially; under it he kicked. He wanted to use Mao Tsetung as a shield. This picture could only have been exposed by putting Mao's words up for debate.

That Lin Piao failed was not the consequence of palace intrigue, but a result of the great mass discussions in China wherein all issues were aired. In this way, his opportunity to get broad political support for his own policies deteriorated. Only intrigue and a coup were left to him and, finally, flight.

The hard and hateful criticisms are really no problem. The Soviet attacks against Mao Tsetung's policies are really hateful. But they are reportedly spread in greater quantities in China than in the Soviet Union. They lack political relevance to China, but they give the Chinese a sense of the opponents' conceptual world.

For many years, campaigns have been launched against bad old habits and against such forms which can prompt incorrect conceptions of the society. Thirteen years back when I was in Liu Lin, the bridal pair for example no longer made obeisance to heaven and earth, but instead to a portrait of Chairman Mao. It was an expression of real and deep respect. But it was a respect which bordered on a cult. This has been criticized and has been done away with for many years.

In the intellectual campaigns and mass discussions, questions are also raised which challenge the conceptions of Mao Tsetung's eternal genius or eternal truths. Who made history? Where do correct ideas come from? Is history formed by geniuses who are born now and then over hundreds of years, and who then bring their truths to the people?

Much of what Mao Tsetung has written or inspired to be written is also the subject of direct debate. His words are openly disputed. He has been a diligent writer who published much of what he wrote under pseudonyms for, among other reasons, just to avoid the outcome of a debate becoming predetermined.

The enormous respect for Mao Tsetung is based on actual conditions. The real question here is not whether someone can get up and swear by Mao Tsetung, but whether his words will have an effect on the great debates in the future or whether they will be turned into empty phrases and general formulas.

What in the end decides this issue is naturally how the discussion will go in the production brigades like Liu Lin. Certainly the respect can become a cult and an authority, authoritarian; if so, then Mao Tsetung's words will no longer have any effect. But I personally do not believe what has been carried out can be undone. When the cork is once extracted from the bottle and the spirits are let loose, when hundreds of millions have accustomed themselves to speaking out and speaking loudly, then it is difficult to put them back into the bottle again and silence the people.

Nevertheless Per Sörbom is right. It is a deeply serious question."

The Express
8/21/75

---

* For more on Liu Lin see:

Jan Myrdal, *Report from a Chinese Village* (New York: Pantheon, 1964); and Myrdal, *China: The Revolution Continued* (New York: Pantheon, 1971).

Main entrance to Liu Lin in northern Shensi Province

Village main street

New housing in foreground stands in sharp contrast to the cave dwellings that dot the mountainside.

Peasant women purchase cloth at village "general store."

Young peasant boy

Children line up for dance at new day nursery.

Fu Hai-tsao, respected village elder

1976

The "Gang of Four" Exposed

The Grief Lies Heavy and Ashen Over the People

China is mourning Mao Tsetung. Out here along the coast of Shantung, the grief is as heavy as in other parts of the country. The last summer has been wonderfully beautiful with clear clean air over the blue ocean, but the grief lies ashen over the people.

Tomorrow, the official mourning week begins. But almost everyone we meet has already put on the black mourning bands. Some have also begun to wear white flowers of sorrow.

There are many department stores and shops in Tsingtao. In the department store on Chungsan Street, which is one of the smaller stores, the sales clerk, Tien Ling-ho, said: "Up to 3:00 P.M. today, we have sold 45,370 mourning arm bands in silk and cotton. This is more than 3,000 meters of material."

Here in Shantung, where there are only evergreen trees, the commemorations are being done up with pine twigs and paper flowers. The big memorial services are being prepared.

In front of all public buildings here in Tsingtao, the flag has been lowered to half mast. Outside the stores and workplaces and throughout the residential quarters, flag masts are being erected to fly mourning flags.

Chairman Mao Tsetung's portrait is draped with black silk.

The grief is heavy, but not overdone. The ceremonies are being kept simple. No "Mao Tsetung Street" nor "Mao Tsetung Square" is found in Tsingtao, much less a "Mao Tsetung Town" in all of China. That decision was made by China's communists at the behest of Mao Tsetung well before the 1949 victory. No one contemplates abandoning that decision.

The national grief is no formality. China is grieving over her greatest son. Many with whom I have spoken still seem numbed by the shock. The news of death struck without their having had any chance to prepare. They only heard it said that a serious announcement would be broadcast on the radio at 4:00 P.M. Then they heard that Chairman Mao Tsetung had passed away just after midnight and that the Party had called for unity. That was yesterday. It still seems that many cannot comprehend that he is really gone.

No one whom I have spoken with here in Tsingtao had received any news at all about Chairman Mao's serious condition. Not even leading cadres in the public administration were prepared for what happened.

"Suddenly came the announcement that he was gone," said Tsingtao's vice-mayor, Chen Kan.

Everyone was well aware of Mao Tsetung's age. They assumed that his health was perhaps not the best, but no one speculated about this. And he had, of course, gotten through so many serious crises before in his life. He had recovered from such hard trials that no one anticipated his departure, not now.

"The news of Chairman Mao Tsetung's departure descended upon us like lightning from a clear sky."

The death comes during a difficult year for China. Many leading statesmen had passed away: Chou En-lai last winter and Chu Teh, last summer, for example. That summer the country was also struck by three serious earthquakes. One of them, in Tangshan, was very serious. The natural catastrophes have taken many lives and caused great injury. Now, out here, for the past few days, there is again warning of a possible earthquake. People have already begun to live in tents, though there is no official sanction of this. But neither panic nor confusion is evident.

There are no supply problems in the country. The harvest is good, and the economy is developing in spite of the strains. The preparedness has subdued the difficulties. But now the Chairman is gone. A hard and resolute grief prevails.

Chairman Mao Tsetung's death comes in the midst of a decisive political showdown in China. This concerns China's future and which course is the correct one. A long period has passed since China pulled herself out of her depths. More than a generation has also passed since the People's Republic was declared at Tien An Men in Peking [Oct. 1, 1949—ed.]. China is now recognized throughout the world as a great and significant country. Her economic development has been magnificent. Here in Tsingtao or far away in the interior, the supply of goods is large and ample.

It has become meaningless to compare China and India the way we still could do ten, fifteen years ago. Now they say: "Do you not see that people wear patched clothes? Almost thirty years have passed since Liberation and we still have not come further. Why should we compare ourselves to India? Why not with Japan? There is still a long way to go."

Chairman Mao Tsetung himself had warned many times against boasting too much of the successes. The people should instead look at the needs and the tasks. But which course is now correct for China?...

Chong Su-ching, an older woman worker in Textile Factory No. 6 in Tsingtao, said: "After hearing the heavy announcement about Chairman Mao Tsetung's passing away, we sat and talked for a long time after work. When I went home, I couldn't sleep. I thought about how it had been.

"Myself, I had been sold twice as a child. Now everything is different. It is to the credit of Chairman Mao Tsetung. He helped us seize power. He is gone now. It is hideous to think. We must transform sorrow into strength which enables us to go on. We have to see to it that no bourgeois mandarins arise in the Party."

In Tsingtao's Middle School No. 17, the twenty-five-year-old woman teacher, Wang Ming huei, wept uncontrollably as I spoke with her. She had been crying very hard and was red-eyed and swollen after a sleepless night. Ten years ago she had been a Red Guard during the Cultural Revolution, one of those millions of Red Guards who had been given responsible posts in work brigades, industries and at schools everywhere in China.

"We were having a study meeting in the class. We were discussing the question of the right deviation and of Teng Hsiao-ping. Then we were told that there would be an important news broadcast on the radio. We did not know what it was about.

"When I heard it said that Chairman Mao Tsetung had passed on, it was as if inside of me the heart and lungs turned to stone. Since then, I have not been able to sleep. Last night I saw before me China's history, all the way from the Opium Wars until now. How wretched we have been, how oppressed, and so many sacrifices! It was Chairman Mao Tsetung who showed us the way to overturn all oppression and all humiliation, and who made it possible for us to build up what we now have. My father participated in the Anti-Japanese War. He was a communist. I was born three years after Chairman Mao Tsetung's proclamation of the People's Republic at Tien An Men Square in Peking. He has been with me all my life. Since the time I was a small child, he has taught me so much.

"It was under his leadership that we young Red Guards staged a revolt during the Great Proletarian Cultural Revolution, when so many new things were created. I myself was among those he received at Tien An Men Square on October 1, 1966. It is not even ten years ago today!

"We swore we would follow his revolutionary line. We promised we would not fear hardship and we would go wherever he indicated. When he encouraged us to go to the countryside and learn from the poor and lower-middle peasants in hard manual work, I made the journey, staunchly determined to stay there for a long time. Then the poor peasants selected me to go to the university to become a teacher of the working people's children.

"Now he is gone. Now the responsibility rests with us. The anguish of his going away is so intense. But I let it burn in me so that it may steel me, so that I can continue his revolutionary line throughout my life in spite of all hardship. This is what I swore when I heard he was no longer with us."

Those who took it hardest were the young people who were just leaving school.

"The first thing I learned to say when I began to talk were the words 'Long Live Chairman Mao!' " says Kao, a seventeen-year-old middle-school pupil.

"Now he is no more. What shall we do? No matter how deeply we grieve for him, he will never come back to life. Our entire class cried when we heard the message. We listened over and over again. In front of his portrait, we promised to study Marxism-Leninism and to be good Red Guards, always following the revolutionary course. It is for sure we of the younger generation who have to take over and carry on the work."

Yes, the Chinese people are grieving over Mao Tsetung. Even old cadres here in Tsingtao have difficulty in not breaking into tears during our talks. I have not been told anything about the conflicts China-watchers speak of from Hong Kong. What I have been told about the future is that it is now necessary to unite and carry on the struggle for Mao Tsetung's line and transform grief into strength. For now the Chairman is gone, and many difficulties await us in the future.

The Express
9/11/76

The Struggle Concerns the Future of 900 Million People

It is very calm here in Tsingtao. As far as I know, it is calm throughout the country. Everywhere people are gathering for meetings and discussions, but there is no uneasiness or excitement. The mood is a most relieved one. Support for the new chairman, Hua Kuo-feng, gives the impression of being honest and very great.

Reports about China often give a false view of reality, but this isn't because journalists lie. Right now I am listening to the Voice of America. The reporting is respectable. It distinguishes between hard facts and rumors which become more and more believable. Then, an expert begins to explain. Afterwards, the listener no longer can comprehend what is happening here in China and why it is happening.

It may seem that China is so mysterious that supernatural

knowledge is needed to understand anything here. But this is not the case. Politics in China is like politics everywhere else, it expresses the real conflicts of real people.

These conflicts in China today do not touch on the relationship with the Soviet leaders. On that issue, the unity among the people is close to 100%. The Kremlin is arming for world war, and Russian efforts at hegemony must be repulsed.

But the present 900 million in socialist China are facing enormous social problems which must be solved. These problems concern the country's future development, and there are different interpretations as to the solutions of these problems. There are also directly conflicting interests. The political struggle in the country has been clearly manifested within the leadership of the state and the Party.

Chairman Mao Tsetung also pointed out time and time again that this was inevitable. Illusions of harmony and lack of conflict are dangerous, for this political struggle is an expression of real social contradictions in Chinese society. The political course is not the business of some leaders. It is of direct and immediate import to the work and daily lives and future of the people. The necessary political struggle therefore has to be consciously carried out by precisely those hundreds of millions so that the country's policies correspond to their interests and needs.

If the social contradictions in China were denied or suppressed, the ruling Communist Party of China would be quickly transformed into a sanctuary for a new upper class, which would rule over the people. The revolutionary phrases would remain, but the Party would turn into a Nazi Party, and China would follow the same course as the Soviet Union.

The reasoning is not difficult to understand. But it explains what the experts are mulling over and why the political discussions in China are constantly so extensive. Struggle between two lines is no empty phrase.

Different political leaders in Peking represent different interests. Through the process of extensive discussions, many of them have been isolated. They have lost their political base. Their views have stood out as phrases in contradiction to the interest of the hundreds of millions.

Certain leading politicians have themselves changed their understanding through the debates. Others have been driven to desperation when they realized they had lost political support. They have taken their refuge in intrigue and maneuvering.

Some politicians who have rapidly risen have shown they are lacking in experience. In China, too, people have distrust for such leaders who, rather than go the long way through daily work with difficult everyday problems and real conflicts, instead have simply taken the elevator toward the top as private secretaries or student politicians.

The political struggle in China is not a private reckoning between a handful of different people. Also, the expressions "radicals" and "moderates" are deceptive when used to characterize the different groups within the Chinese leadership. It is neither a matter of a palace revolution, though certain people were gripped with desperation in the final showdown, nor of a "left" which has now lost a power struggle within the leadership.

It concerns an intensive political struggle in which hundreds of millions of people have participated over the last few years. The crucial decisions regarding certain persons have been made in the course of the past year, not during the past weeks.

It was Chairman Mao Tsetung who initiated that extensive political settlement on the line of further construction of China, and he also led the discussion until his last illness.

Step by step, the issue of correct selections was investigated. Following the death of Premier Chou En-lai, Hua Kou-feng was first appointed Provisional Premier, at the suggestion of Chairman Mao Tsetung, and then appointed to full Premier and First Vice Party Chairman.

He was then elected Party Chairman after Mao Tsetung's departure, assigned the task of carrying on the past policy of the Party.

The Express
10/17/76

Mass Meetings Decide China's Future

- By 1980, China's agriculture will for the most part be mechanized. At the turn of the century, socialist China will be among the world's economically developed countries.
- At the same time that the people's livelihood is improved, the social and economic gaps will be reduced.
- The Party will not be able, as in the Soviet Union, to develop into a ruling class of privileged people which for the sake of its own interests exercises dictatorship over the people.
- Neither will China participate in the superpowers' struggle for world domination. It will not try to gain supremacy over other countries, nor will it build up an offensive military force.
- The policies of maintaining a strong preparedness against war and natural catastrophes by means of a vastly expanded people's defense will continue. Neither Russian nor other overlords will be given any chance of exercising any influence over China.

These are some of the guiding principles which resulted from the enormous mass discussions which were carried out during the past years in China under Mao Tsetung's initiative. Mao Tsetung built great unity around these goals; and Chou En-lai was therefore able to formulate this unity into practical working tasks for socialist China at the Fourth National People's Congress.

These perspectives explain the great relief with which an overwhelming majority here in China greeted Hua Kuo-feng's election as chairman of the Party. This overwhelming majority views that selection as a confirmation that the basic policies which they see as correct will be carried out. Some minority will not succeed in altering the course.

The last year here has been a year of intensive political struggle. Bitter and desperate attempts to abandon past decisions or change their content have been made from different directions. This political struggle has not been played out behind the closed doors of a meeting room in Peking. It has taken place this year at millions of meetings all over the country.

Everywhere, in Party organizations and at study meetings, in factories and offices, in agricultural work and in schools, people have sat up until late at night and thrashed out the issues.

The discussions have been hard and trying. Attempts to throw out decisions or to change their meaning have not always been presented in a manner which is straightforward and to the point. But the political course is a matter of concern for all. What political reality is hidden behind this or that issue?

It is not a matter of empty ritualistic meetings with formal discourses. There have been times when it really got hot. This spring, oblique attacks were made on the late Chou En-lai. He had formulated many of the correct goals which the great majority of China had affirmed during the debates Mao Tsetung had introduced and carried out. Although dead, Chou En-lai still stood in the way of those who wanted to alter the course. Their attempts and insinuations unleashed a strong response.

This spring and summer, the political struggle grew more acute. At the same time, real issues became clearer and clearer. This was also revealed as Hua Kuo-feng was chosen Provisional Premier and First Vice Party Chairman. His selection took place under the advice of Mao Tsetung. The attempts to extend the campaign against Teng Hsiao-ping to even interfere directly with the decisions of the Fourth National People's Congress had failed.

Those who tried to basically alter China's policies exposed themselves more and more as an isolated minority. This minority, however, dominated important positions within the Party and state, from which they could maneuver. But the political base for those positions became hollower by the day.

The minority larded their speeches with super-revolutionary phrases. But during these years, people had learned to thrash out questions. They now demanded proof and arguments. One could, of course, make revolution in women's fashions too and propose that the dress of the Tang Dynasty be the festive dress for China's women on special occasions. But people really knew how it was.

In Shanghai and in Peking, families can contemplate buying a TV if both man and wife are working at skilled jobs. But in the brigades out in the countryside, the cash remuneration for a grown man's hard day's work is still very low. The gaps are still real ones.

It is possible to achieve the goals of the Fourth National People's Congress. China's people can carry out the task by their own efforts in the way Mao Tsetung has shown. But additional great efforts will be required. Rhetoric will not help.

With Chairman Mao Tsetung's death, the political conflict became really acute. A new Party chairman had to be appointed and all signs pointed to Hua Kuo-feng.

The minority saw no possibility of having their candidate selected to the post. At the same time, their political base was eroding, and representatives of the minority began to appear more and more clearly as people who exploited the revolution's words to achieve power.

They had also made use of their positions to manipulate Mao Tsetung's speeches and instructions of the past years to their own advantage. Ideas had been taken out of context. This could not be concealed much longer. The minority then switched to desperate and extreme attempts to force a solution which would be advantageous to their interests. They did not succeed. Hua Kuo-feng is Party Chairman. The goal of the Fourth National People's Congress remains in force, and Mao Tsetung's works will also be published in their entirety.

If relief over the outcome is great, then the bitterness

towards the minority's leading persons is no less great. It is not odd that there will now be widespread demonstrations against them.

For within the Communist Party, the minority did not find support. During the great discussions, it had also been rejected by an overwhelming majority of China's people. The minority could only seize power in the Party by coup and high-handed attempts to remove representatives of the majority. Had the minority succeeded in carrying this out, then the Party's character would have also been basically altered.

The minority would have then been able to realize its exercise of power over China only by setting up a dictatorship of a few over the people against the outspoken wishes of the overwhelming majority. This would in all probability have led to armed struggle and civil war. Such a regime would have been regarded as illegal in many circles. And the people are armed in China.

A regime without popular support, which comes into open struggle with its own people, must seek support where it can get it. The possibilities are thus opened to foreign intrusion in China's affairs.

It is incorrect, I believe, to call this group "the left" or "the radicals" of China. Its revolutionary rhetoric cannot conceal the fact that to achieve power, this group played with China's future. It did so in such a way that the people's bitterness against them here in this country is very understandable.

The Express
10/21/76

The Real Left and the Spurious One

There has not been a struggle between "left" forces around Chiang Ching and "rightist" forces around Chou En-lai which has now been decided by Hua Kuo-feng to the advantage of the right.

But there has been struggle between right and left, and that struggle has been carried out by the great masses in this country of 900 million.

It can be said that the central figures in this political struggle over China's future have been Chou En-lai and Chiang Ching, and that Hua Kuo-feng is now carrying on Chou En-lai's work. But Chou En-lai was no rightist force.

It has been said that the struggle regarded the inheritance of Mao Tsetung. This is one way it may be put. Chairman Mao Tsetung was old, and even if it was not expected that he would pass away so soon, the question of his successor was of immediate importance. But the issue of succession was not so much about this or that post, as it was about continuing Chairman Mao's work.

Chiang Ching had been married for almost forty years to Chairman Mao. Chou En-lai and Mao Tsetung had worked together for a long time and, since the Chinese Communist Party had fixed its course in 1935, these two had been in leadership of the Party and the state. They had complemented one another in the same remarkable way that Marx and Engels once had.

Chiang Ching tried to make political capital of her marriage to Chairman Mao Tsetung, but their marriage had not been good for a long time. Mao Tsetung was obliged to point out that Chiang Ching spoke for herself and not for him; he was disturbed by her political ambitions and warned her against intriguing and building cliques around herself. Chiang Ching and Chou En-lai were both politically active, both in positions of responsibility, and both had personal ties to Mao Tsetung for a long time. But it was Chou En-lai and Mao Tsetung who worked closely together, and Chou En-lai's speeches expressed this common political standpoint. As far as Chiang Ching's speeches were concerned, however, they only expressed her own standpoint.

On the question of an immediate successor, Mao Tsetung had had this to say in spring 1976. At his suggestion, Hua Kuo-feng had been selected as Premier and been given the newly-created post of First Vice Party Chairman. Hua Kuo-feng had worked for a long time at different levels. He had accepted responsibility for local as well as national questions. Mao Tsetung had expressed confidence in his ability to master the real and enormous problems China faces.

It is around the solution to these problems that the struggle has revolved. This is why it became so deep-going and extensive. It has not been a question of individuals, though such questions were not unimportant. The people are the driving force in history, but this fact does not do away with the need for leaders. In certain situations, the question of who has the highest posts can become completely decisive.

This explains the enormous relief and happiness in China when the political battles, which lasted a long time and involved masses of people, were finally resolved. The "gang of four" were removed from all their posts and made politically harmless. This is an important point, and I will come back to it.

Since Liberation, China's people have lifted the country out of deepest misery through enormous effort. Now China has made great progress. Socialist China is working with space research and nuclear physics. But socialist China is still a developing country of the third world. Almost thirty years have passed since Liberation, but there are still many who go in patched and tattered clothes. They do not do so because they are "puritans" or "moralists" or "sloppy," or because they would not like to do otherwise. They do so because the material resources are still not sufficient to ensure all of China's 900 million people a good living standard.

They have come a long way. It is hardly possible to compare the situation today with the misery of yesterday. There is a basic security now. No one is starving, no one lacks clothing. School is compulsory, and educational opportunities are opening up.

One can now begin to say that almost every family has been able to procure the "four bigs": bicycle, transistor radio, sewing machine and watch. Even the department stores deep in

China's interior are filled with goods. In the large cities, the "four bigs" are fast becoming the "five bigs": bicycle, transistor radio, sewing machine, watch and television. But in spite of all this, economic differences in the country are still great and income gaps are marked.

For their work, the members of the communes receive in part a basic provision of grain and in part cash, or the equivalent. I have been to brigades where this income matches or even supersedes the industrial workers'. But I have also been to brigades where a full grown man's day's work cannot bring in enough money to buy a pack of Chunghua, the Chinese filtered cigarettes foreigners cherish. He has to stick to much simpler brands if he is a smoker.

Chinese policies deal with reducing these differences. This is absolutely necessary, since these differences are constantly breeding new and privileged groups who tend to go the same way as those with privileges or in power went in the Soviet Union. This is what makes the different campaigns against bourgeois right so necessary.

But these campaigns cannot do away with the differences. They can only limit them. For goods are lacking. These goods can only be created through work. To build up production so that it can satisfy the people's material needs is a protracted and difficult job. During all this time, shortages, and hence differences, will prevail, constantly breeding new groups seeking to preserve their privileges. There will be many debates in the future in China. A hard grip must be kept on the revolution in order to promote production. If production is not promoted, all rhetoric of revolution will become only empty words. Words do not feed anyone.

During and after the Cultural Revolution's great changes, these issues have been discussed in great detail in all of China. What began as catchword sloganeering of Mao Tsetung's quotations has become independent studies of political classics. Mao Tsetung sought to get a basic political discussion under way in the country, one which was both broad and deep. During these discussions much unity was gradually achieved around Mao Tsetung's line for China, and it was also ratified programmatically at the Tenth Party Congress and the Fourth National People's Congress. The documents, giving the direction and ratified by the congresses, had been worked out in close collaboration with Chairman Mao Tsetung.

Chou En-lai's reports to the Tenth Party Congress and Fourth National People's Congress were developed together with Mao Tsetung. The domestic and foreign political course drawn up there has been ratified by the congresses and is in effect. The plan of China's construction and modernization, which Chou En-lai proposed at the Fourth National People's Congress in January 1975, had been worked out together with Mao Tsetung. After nationwide debate, it has been ratified by the Party's and state's highest policy-making organs. This deserves to be emphasized. For right after those decisions, something odd began to occur.

Within the country, the decisions of the Fourth National People's Congress were downplayed. Instead of revisionists, empiricists (those who base themselves solely on facts at hand) suddenly became targets of attack in the press and mass media. Vague and frothy articles were published.

China-watchers all over the world also began to have access to different internal Chinese documents. They began to write that the "left" in China was now reacting to the "right course," represented by Chou En-lai. They were often very well informed on different questions of detail. Those writings of 1975 and 1976 undermined China's reputation, fomented an uncertainty about China's policy and contributed to confusing some of China's friends. It seemed as if open channels went from the organs of the central government and Party in Peking straight to China-watchers in Hong Kong.

Mao Tsetung was very old and Chou En-lai deathly ill, and, throughout the country, strange things were happening. The "gang of four" was preparing to take power after the Chairman.* All of them had attained leading positions during the

* See gang note, p. 3.

Cultural Revolution. Mao Tsetung had harbored great hopes for the young Wang Hung-wen from Shanghai and even helped Yao Wen-yuan in his writing. The "gang of four" was responsible for the mass media, art and literature. The four readily tried to put themselves forward as if they were special representatives of the Cultural Revolution. The expansion of the medical services with barefoot doctors and all the other big reforms made during and after the Cultural Revolution were made out to be their doing.

This was simply not true. They had had propagandistic tasks during the Cultural Revolution. But it was an enormous mass movement which Mao Tsetung himself had initiated. Chou En-lai had had responsibility for the practical work and for ensuring that the state was kept intact during the period.

Already during the Cultural Revolution, the "gang of four" was dimly seen in odd contexts. Mao Tsetung pointed out that there were bad aspects to the Cultural Revolution. Slogans appeared such as "Down with Everything!" Methods of violence rather than persuasion were used against those with different views. Instead of saying that the overwhelming majority of cadres were good or fairly good, certain groups began to say that the overwhelming majority of cadres were bad. Here and there debates became what Mao Tsetung called "full-fledged civil war." Open fascist, counter-revolutionary incidents, such as the burning of the British legation, were presented as revolt.* Students who shot at workers called themselves revolutionaries. This was not the Cultural Revolution; it was the Cultural Revolution's counter-revolutionaries, and the great mass movement during the period also swept away this self-annointed "real left."

While in the limelight, the gang's intentions were only dimly perceived. Yao Wen-yuan and Chang Chun-chiao were responsible for strange slogans; Chiang Ching had coarsely

* In August 1967, a group of students burned the British mission in Peking. They did this in defiance of Chou En-lai and other Chinese leaders who ordered them to stop their activities.

inflamed the youth to take up arms. During a tumultuous period, these could have been seen as the indiscreet remarks of propagandists. Precisely such indiscreet remarks and lack of judgment made it impossible for them to be able to fill a Chou En-lai's or much less a Mao Tsetung's role. But they had also been found close to Lin Piao and had worked together with him, and he had promoted Chiang Ching to her prominent position. But when he was ultimately exposed by Chou En-lai and nothing else remained for him but a hasty flight, Chiang Ching and the others then scurried to portray themselves as his victims.

But it could appear that they represented some sort of pseudo-left, a flighty and giddy "left" of various intellectuals and certain youth. Wang Hung-wen was also often portrayed as a spokesperson for the youth and for the new generation, and he very early was given significant and responsible duties. But he did not handle them successfully and did not fulfill the expectations Mao Tsetung had for him.

Nothing is really unusual about this. In every organization, there are people who are chosen to boards who then do not live up to expectations. Sometimes they disappear after a while from the board's work, and sometimes they succeed in improving their work and can later take on important tasks. Each and every one of us who has worked in organizations knows this. The same conditions, though with unbelievably greater burdens of responsibility, holds true within the leadership of China's Communist Party. Mao Tsetung's line was always to try to help such leaders correct their work. Only in very extreme cases was one to give up hope. That meant that Mao Tsetung made a very great effort to convince, for example, the Seventh and Eighth Party Congresses to select to the Central Committee even representatives who had made serious mistakes and who had been the object of very harsh political criticism.

For the same reasons, Mao Tsetung made a clear-cut distinction between political deviation and direct criminality. Whoever now visits the locale in Shanghai where China's

Communist Party was founded in 1921 can get a very careful explanation of who participated in it and what later became of their policies. There is a survivor from the Party's founding who now lives in China and is quite old. It is Liu Jen-ching, who organized the Trotskyite movement in 1927 and who was therefore expelled from the Party in 1929. He was a political opportunist, an active enemy of the Party. After Liberation, he got a job as a white-collar worker in a publishing house in Peking. He is now living there on a pension. This is one of the proud traditions of China's Communist Party, to distinguish between crime and political struggle. Liu Shao-chi was politically exposed, but he disappeared completely from the scene when his past was investigated, and it was found he had had very shady dealings.... Teng Hsiao-ping, who had also committed serious errors, did not have such marks in his past and was later reinstated....

Those four people, Chang Chun-chiao, Chiang Ching, Yao Wen-yuan and Wang Hung-wen, would not, however, accept this. They were rather isolated in the Party's leadership, and it gradually became clear that they had formed their own little group. Mao Tsetung was disturbed about this. He warned them against getting isolated and working against the Party. He also became seriously disturbed by Chiang Ching's conduct. She had really no function in the state. At the same time, she intrigued to meet with foreign heads of state and dignitaries.

"Chiang Ching seems to have gotten wild ambitions," said Mao Tsetung. The ambitions were, however, wilder than one might have initially thought. The "gang of four" formed a group to take over the state and the Party. Its members saw that Chou En-lai was deathly ill and that Mao Tsetung was very old. They believed they could make use of their power over the mass media and their influence over the country to seize power. Prior to the Fourth National People's Congress, they made a move to get Chou En-lai out of the way. That failed.

After that Congress, the gang then launched an intensive

political campaign in the country to get support for their plans. Its members made use of different channels abroad, and suddenly China began to leak information like a sieve. Not always correct information and not especially useful for the country's political credibility, but useful for the "gang of four," who by international measure began to appear as the representatives of the left and the Cultural Revolution's gains. Their political base inside the country was very small.

One can certainly say that the gang's roots were mostly in certain sections of the theater and music world, among journalists and mass media people, among certain student groups, in the sports fields and at some hospitals. This is not much base for a real left, and neither is it a base for a serious attempt at political power in the state. The "gang of four" then began to make serious use of their power over the mass media and over their channels to gather a social group about them which could serve as a base for a planned attempt to seize state power. Its members thereby followed the same path as Lin Piao had earlier and could only generate support on the same grounds. Instead of maybe having represented a left tendency, they began shaping a fascist and elitist force on the basis of those tendencies which are petty bourgeois, support privilege and which are continuously arising in China. There, the differences can still only be limited; but production is not sufficient to meet all of the people's needs and is not thus sufficient to become the basis for ending the real lack of equality. In contrast to Lin Piao, none of these four had ever been a real hero who made contributions through real struggle. Even after his fall and his cowardly flight, there is still in history a real contribution which is Lin Piao's.

Within the Party's highest leadership, Chang Chung-chiao therefore took up the struggle directly against the decisions of the Fourth National People's Congress. He made his attack from the "left," warning that an increase in production would lead to capitalism.

"What's the use of this or that many tons of steel or grain?" he asked. "Look at the Soviet Union! Stalin worked to increase production and now the Soviet Union has satellites in the sky, but the red flag lies prostrate on the ground." This sounded revolutionary and the subsequent slogans were obvious.

Certainly it was not steel production in the thirties which led to the Soviet Union's going fascist today; rather it made it possible for the Soviet Union to withstand Hitler's attack.

Now Mao Tsetung stepped in and warned against Chang Chun-chiao's line. Empiricism was not the main danger; it was revisionism. But the "gang of four" gathered their forces throughout the country to go on the offensive. Wang Hung-wen traveled around to organize the struggle in the factories. In official speeches, he appeared as the Central Committee's representative and spoke of unity; while in private discussions, he drew up the guidelines on how the gang would build a fighting "left opposition."

Throughout China the struggle became very intense. At all meetings and in all Party organizations, people sat up until late at night. What was true and what false? What was left and not left? Teng Hsiao-ping made political mistakes and was criticized, and the "gang of four" tried to exploit the occasion to go against the Central Committee's decision on the campaign. They made the demand that all of "Teng's men" at the local level should be ousted and all "Teng's protectors" should be attacked. They also tried to label Teng a criminal and not a person who had committed political errors. By going against Mao Tsetung's and the Central Committee's instructions in this way, the gang tried to make a pretext for a nationwide "rectification" campaign against all Party cadres who stood for the Party's line.

In the industries and factories where they succeeded in winning some support, the "gang of four" took advantage of the fact that incomes are guaranteed in socialist China. They especially won over many young students who had just come into production with their line that revolution and production are in opposition. These students continued to collect their monthly wage, though they ceased going to their workplaces. The "gang of four" encouraged this and called it revolutionary.

These groups also picked up support from some of the older people. They drew up the slogan that it was wrong to work for revisionists. By this, they meant that they would not do work in those companies where they could not seize power. At the same time, they collected their wages.

Inside the transportation sector, the gang raised the slogan: "Follow the straight revolutionary road; crush the revisionist exactness." During the spring of 1975 and the spring and summer of 1976, many industries stopped producing, train timetables could not be followed. Here and there near-serious accidents occurred.

China was not able to fulfill its production plan. In the export industries, there were many orders which could not be filled. China lost two years, and the people's living standards were not improved. Here and there, supplies of provisions got worse.

Among the students, the "gang of four" agitated that every form of proficiency review was reactionary. Among the youth as a whole, they agitated that the struggle concerned "the young against the old." Only the youth could be revolutionary. All the time, the payments of monthly wages and allowances continued, irrespective of whether the recipients really worked or not. The older workers or regular young people who felt that this was shameful parasitism were labeled counter-revolutionaries. Here and there they went into fighting violently with clubs and whips against those persistent old "capitalist roaders" who "placed production above revolution," that is to say, workers who carried out production work.

It was completely clear that this did not have anything to do with socialism or the left. This was typical petty bourgeois anarchism. It expressed the petty bourgeoisie's desire to ensure its own privileged status against the working people and at the expense of the working people.

This was carried out in the name of the Cultural Revolution, but had nothing to do with it. The working people of China, who know the country's real needs and who know that no industry can continue to pay wages to those who refuse to participate in production, felt great bitterness towards the gang and its followers. Many were disturbed. Had this situation continued, the people would have had to live off roots and leaves within a few years.

The "gang of four" exploited the real and great freedom of expression which China's constitution grants. Many cities were filled with wall newspapers which encouraged revolt. In Shanghai, the "gang of four" tried to form a base which could be directly used against the state. There, they believed, they had control over the Party and the people's militia and military power. Their control over the mass media gave them a false sense of security. With the advent of the great earthquakes, Chang and Yao wrote poems of how the earth trembled and the heavens split open before the ascension of a new dynasty. The crisis became severe with the Chairman's death. At that time, the gang falsified a statement by Mao Tsetung in a letter to Hua Kuo-feng that one should follow the Party's tradition and created "Mao's testament": "Follow the principles laid down." They had substituted three characters to make it sound like an imperial edict.

When Hua Kuo-feng confronted them with facts and proved they had falsified Mao Tsetung's words, the gang was panic-stricken. On October 4, 1976, they called for struggle against the Party and government. They attacked Hua Kuo-feng for pursuing the capitalist road and betraying Mao Tsetung, and they predicted a dark destiny for him. This was the signal to their followers. But they had no time left, for Hua Kuo-feng and the Central Committee stepped in. And when the gang's trusted people in Shanghai, who had already written the call to the people of the world and distributed weapons and ammunition, called Peking on their private lines, there was no answer. And none of their followers poured out into the streets to support them. The gang had no masses behind them. They were arrested by the very people's militia they had armed and mobilized for their coup.

Now there is widespread rejoicing. But the people do not mention those youth drawn into the struggle against production. They were misled. The older workers are now explaining to them that he who does not work, neither shall he eat, and that this applies to young people as well as older people, companies as well as states. In China, they are now trying to catch up on the missed years. They are keeping a firm grip on the revolution to be able to increase production and thus to continue the struggle against privileges and bourgeois right until the people's material needs can be satisfied and the differences can be completely eliminated.

The People in Pictures/ Cultural Front
No. 22/1976

The Day All the Brandy in Tsingtao Was Drunk Up

The day it became evident that the "gang of four" had been defeated, all the brandy in Tsingtao was drunk up. China has the most sober of traditions, but that day people throughout the country drank to their fill.

When the news was confirmed, one of my friends became so excited and joyful that she had a heart attack and had to be hospitalized.

For four days, the people of Tsingtao demonstrated. Drums were beaten, firecrackers were lit and large meetings were held. By that time, in the autumn of 1976, the members of the "gang of four" had become the most feared and despised politicians in China. The relief over their fall was tremendous.

The defeat of the "gang of four" is one of the most important events of China's history since 1949. This is significant not only for the countries of Asia, but also for us in Europe and America.

China is no monolithic unit. There is political struggle in China, and it is naturally in the end a struggle on issues which concern the work and daily lives of the people. The "gang of four" are often called "radical" or "left" outside of China. But this means that one can speak of a political left which goes against the interests of the overwhelming majority.

To call it "left" is as unreasonable as to say that the regime which is kept in power in East Berlin with Russian bayonets actually expresses the interests of the working class. A minority which tries to rule against and over the people is reactionary. This is the way the vast majority in China also regard the "gang of four."

When Hua Kuo-feng and the Central Committee acted against the "gang of four," they reaffirmed the policies decided upon at the various congresses and represented by Chou En-lai. Those policies had been formulated together with Mao Tsetung. Policies are to serve the people.

This meant a rapid economic development by one's own force, improved living standards, diminished inequality, an expanded educational system, concern for the elderly and sick, as well as law and order.

The latter is not unimportant. The "gang of four" abrogated freedom of expression and democracy by branding each and every one who opposed them as a reactionary or capitalist roader or even a counter-revolutionary. They encouraged their groups to use fascist methods and attack people.

But the Chinese people have not made revolution to be attacked or gagged when they speak. They demand that those decisions found in the constitution for protection of privacy, of personal integrity, and of security of rights be respected by everyone, as Chou En-lai had said. In China, it is not only forbidden to attack people, but also to install eavesdropping equipment in their homes.

Had the "gang of four" succeeded in seizing power, they would have been forced to turn their shirts inside out and set up a harsh terroristic dictatorship of a minority in order to ensure their rule.

Their foreign policy would have been shaped accordingly. They would have collaborated with Soviet leaders to run wild in South Asia. The Soviet pressure on Europe would have increased and China would have become an aggression-prone superpower in Asia. It is not without reason that the relief over the defeat of the "gang of four" is so great all over Asia.

This is what my friends in China said when the "gang of four" fell. But the "gang of four" were also despised and looked down upon as individuals.

The gang was hypocritical. They had climbed to power with high-sounding moralizing. They had fought everything which normal people considered fun. They had condemned card playing and forbidden the kinds of music that people liked. They had labeled those who had goldfish or potted plants as reactionary and bourgeois. All this they had done in the name of revolution. Yet gang members themselves went to restaurants and ate and drank lavishly while the state carried the tab. And afterwards, they watched privately imported films. This was widely talked about.

Wang Hung-wen's interest in automobiles was recounted: he had acquired nouveau riche mannerisms and become a real little Brezhnev. He only wanted to travel faster and faster in nicer and nicer cars, but he couldn't drive. He was not even good for that.

The "gang of four" was feared and despised and scorned. Had they succeeded in the autumn of 1976 in carrying out their plans to seize power in China, they would have unleashed a bloody civil war.

The Express
12/26/76

On the Settlement with the "Gang of Four"

Mao Tsetung always had a very clear line on cadres who have made mistakes. It was not the individual, but the political line which should be fought. For example, prior to the election of the Central Committee, as well as the Seventh and Eighth Party Congresses, he made great efforts to recommend people who had earlier stood for views which had been severely criticized. He tried to the very last to win the "gang of four" over to the right side. He also urged: "Don't function as a gang of four. . . . Why don't you unite with the more than 200 Members óf the Central Committee of the Party?"*

This manner of handling political contradictions inside leading organs is not so remarkable, but some in the mass media have speculated and made Pekingology out of it....

The direct cause of the fall of the "gang of four" can be found in their different intrigues to seize power within the Party and state. In China, it does not pay to say that one is an opponent of Mao Tsetung. In that case, no one would get support. The "gang of four" thus waved the red flag and presented themselves as super-revolutionaries.

Take the example of proficiency tests. This shows how the gang worked. They took up a correct issue: the struggle against the old mandarin system in education, the grade chase and careerism. They ostensibly threw themselves behind Mao Tsetung's view. But later, the four twisted and distorted things until the gang, in typically petty bourgeois fashion, fought every form of proficiency review. "Revolutionaries do not need proficiency tests," it was said. They called this "Fighting Book Worship," though the social background of such demands is actually very clear. It is a line which benefits neither the working class nor the poor peasants, but the members of small middle groups who seek to attain lucrative posts without having to strain themselves. The working people are against the mandarin system, but they have requirements for proficiency. The "gang of four's" line on the issue of grades shows what kind of radicalism theirs was, parasitic petty bourgeois radicalism!...

Within industry, they twisted politics around in the same way. "Put politics in command," they shouted. It sounded right. But the gang then converted these politics into words only. For their supporters, the working hours were transformed into sessions of revolutionary gabbing. This is much less demanding than participating in production.

The "revolutionary groups" thus formed could receive

* *Documents of the Eleventh National Congress of the Communist Party of China* (Peking: Foreign Languages Press, 1977), p. 15.

wages without having to exert themselves in work. In China, wages are guaranteed. Even if the factory stops production, wages are paid to the workers. This could have ended in catastrophe. As the class-conscious workers said: "We could have been forced to live off the grass."

These different anarchistic actions were not expressions of some working class struggle. Small groups lead them. The. "gang of four" exploited these petty bourgeois anarchistic groups to maneuver their way to power. Had they been successful, it would have quickly meant the end of every form of action by the workers; not only the end to the anarchistic actions, but also to the possibility of workers acting politically on the factory floor. The working class in China has the constitutional right to take to the strike weapon. The settlement with the "gang of four" ensures that right.

Mao Tsetung exhorted taking a firm grip on the revolution to promote production. The gang turned this inside out by contending that production takes care of itself, provided that one busies oneself with revolution. Every working person knows there would be neither revolution nor production, only empty words. As a political line, however, it means that career possibilities are open to the phrasemongers.

My Chinese friends spoke a lot of this struggle in industry. It evoked important questions which had to be thoroughly discussed. It had been shown, they pointed out, that material incentives in production lead to revisionism and prepare the way for capitalism. At the same time, the working person had to receive payment according to work performance, and the graduated wage scale was still applicable. Where should the line be drawn?

In China it is said that the "gang of four" and its followers only comprised a handful. This may seem surprising. But one has to remember that a handful in China can be a great many in absolute numbers. Suppose that the gang had support of as many as one percent of China's people. This means eight or nine million, if you include old as well as young people. It is important to bear these proportions in mind.

Whether it was a matter of one percent or a little more or less, the support the gang had did not fall from the sky. There are differences in China. It will take many years of hard work in production to create the means to abolish what has been termed "bourgeois right." During that long period, as Mao Tsetung so carefully emphasized in continuation of Lenin and Marx, it is only possible to limit these differences, these bourgeois rights. But from out of these conditions, new petty bourgeois currents are continuously reborn. The "gang of four" gathered strength from them.

Of course, some supported the gang. We traveled around China, and we also stayed in rebel headquarters, such as in Chengtu. But those who supported the "gang of four" are not the principal enemies of the Chinese people, and they are not treated as such. It is, the Chinese communists say, incorrect to direct the blow against the many. The gang tried to mislead their young rebels to attack with violent and fascist methods the class-conscious workers who maintained production. The "gang of four" has now been toppled. It is not within the working class that the struggle should be continued. These "rebels" are not to be punished; revenge is not to be taken on them. The issues are to be cleared up through discussion. The heavy blows are to be aimed against the "gang of four" and the handful who comprised their tools and agents.

Indeed, the gang did have a certain amount of political support from a small minority who, in absolute numbers, was not insignificant; but it was only a handful who really tried to carry out the gang's line and who are now to be struggled against directly. . . .

The "gang of four" was especially powerful within the cultural sphere. But it was not always on issues of principle that the gang went to attack. They tried to transform their sphere of influence into a monopoly for themselves and their friends. They worked like Lin Piao, trying to build up a network of people who were bound to them through favors and personal ties. The gang favored their own. Whoever yelled loudly on their behalf advanced without having to do much.

There were a number of questions of principle. Among them was the "gang of four's" sham line on youth: not only "young is beautiful," but "young is best," "young is revolutionary." This meant the old cadres were described as bad, stifflegged and old-fashioned. It was therefore their obligation to leave everything to the youth. In this way, the gang tried to solicit support among the youth. They attempted to set up a centralized leadership of youth organizations which could disseminate such thoughts and, at the same time, serve as a second center in the state.

This line on youth is in and of itself not radical. Slogans attaching political importance to questions of generation are often questionable. During the sixties, the "revolt" of those in Europe and the United States who contended that youth "couldn't trust anyone over thirty" was a revolt shaped by the mass media and fashion industry. This revolt tried to channel social upheaval in a manner economically profitable to monopoly capital, into private revolt. ("The bourgeoisies in your countries have learned a few things since 1917," commented one of my Chinese friends.) Hitler's seizure of power was in his time called the "revolt of the German youth," and the party song of the Italian fascists was called "Youth." In asserting that the real contention was between young and old, the gang had thus formulated in ideological terms a clearly reactionary political line.

The similarity between the "gang of four's" line on youth and certain youth and feminist ideologies in the United States is scarcely coincidental. The gang took a lot of inspiration from there.

Take the film *The Pioneers,* for example. The gang attacked it. The film was not done by their friends. It is, if taken on its own merits, not the world's best film; but, in general, it is good. It also contains parts which are even very good from a technical standpoint. The film follows a worker from the period before Liberation up to the present time. After Liberation, he participates in the construction of the oil fields in Taching. At the end of the film, he is a middle-aged man. It was the opinion of the "gang of four" that he should die a tragic and painful hero's death in the middle of the film, so that a young hero would get the chance to carry on the construction work.

The "gang of four" contended that they themselves had created the modern Peking Opera. This is not true, but their political line was reflected in the showing of those operas: in the out of proportion and unchangeable heroic figures and in the formalized and ritualistic style. There is much good in the new Peking Opera, which now seeks to depict contemporary, common working people, while before, emperors, courtesans and demons dominated the scene. But there are also incorrect tendencies which have gained considerable influence. One example is the use of traditional music to mark the negative. All Chinese people recognize their traditional music, love and appreciate it. But the gang suppressed much traditional music and misused its motif. During the summer of 1976, I saw many of the song and dance pieces which the gang had promoted. It was quite noticeable that the young heroes in them constantly danced on their toes to a kind of Western music. When the villain then came creeping in, he was masked as in old Peking Opera and moved about according to the old opera manner, performing his acrobatic leaps to traditional Chinese music. This turned the audience's experiences inside out.

I then discussed the question very extensively with my Chinese friends. They contended, and this was many months before the gang was ousted, that this was an incorrect and harmful distortion. Many of them indicated that this caused the audience to yearn for the villain and to view the young hero dancing on his toes with tired desperation. There were those who worshipped everything foreign and who did not have respect for the people and who had acquired much power, they said, without, however, disclosing names.

There have also been hard struggles in other cultural areas, in connection with archeological exhibits, for instance. The gang broke with Mao Tsetung's line that the old shall serve the new. One can see the large archeological exhibitions as an attack upon the "gang of four's" attempt to maintain total control over cultural life. Especially in the cultural area, the struggle between the two lines has been bitter and harsh during the past years, as the gang tried to make use of its political power in this realm to try to capture leadership of the Party and state....

Teng Hsiao-ping committed errors. But to serve its own interests, the gang tried to take over the campaign against him to change it and alter its direction. They did this in three ways:

They did this in part by presenting him as a criminal, a counter-revolutionary like Lin Piao. The Chinese Communist Party has always made a clear distinction between political errors and counter-revolution. Political errors, even serious political acts, are not crimes.

China's Communist Party has also made a clear distinction between what belongs to history and what is current. Whoever has committed an error should have the opportunity to change.

Teng Hsiao-ping, as well as Liu Shao-chi, was sharply criticized during the Cultural Revolution. But when their pasts were investigated and old newspaper files and documents examined, it became apparent the two were very different. There were bad marks in Liu Shao-chi's past. There was nothing similar in Teng Hsiao-ping's past. He could therefore return to responsible tasks after he had made self-criticisms. But he then committed new political errors. The most serious was that he did not accept the Cultural Revolution's judgment against him. He was criticized for this. But he was not expelled from the Party. This is an important point. Mao Tsetung regarded him not as a criminal, but as a person who had made political errors. But the gang tried here to distort the Party's line and to obscure the line of distinction between political errors and crimes. They did this with their own ends in mind.

In part, the gang also broke with the instructions of the Central Committee to criticize Teng Hsiao-ping's political errors but not to take up the struggle at the local level. Instead, they said, "Pick out the people who supported Teng, the right deviationists throughout the country." They tried to set in

motion attacks on the great majority of the Party's leading
cadres. This meant striking against the many. It was a repeat of
the incorrect line Yao Wen-yuan had represented during the
Cultural Revolution. Chairman Mao Tsetung's line was that
the great majority of cadres were good or maybe good; theirs
was that the great majority of cadres were bad. Throughout
China they tried to divert the campaign against Teng Hsiao-
ping's political errors to strike against the good local cadres,
who, through hard and self-sacrificing work, correctly
carried out the decisions of the Fourth National People's
Congress and the Tenth Party Congress. The decisions for
China's development representing the line of Mao Tsetung and
Chou En-lai and the entire Party began to be attacked by the
gang. They struck against the many to protect the few. In this
way, they tried to clear the way for their own conquest of
power.

Finally, they contended it was necessary to attack the high
official who stood behind Teng. In freer language, this meant
they tried to divert the campaign and target Chou En-lai. They
tried to present the Premier as a great mandarin. In this way,
the gang was trying to subvert the memory of Chou En-lai and
to undermine his great influence. Chou En-lai stood for the
line of the Party and the state, and, for a long time, he had
represented Mao Tsetung's politics. Even after his death, he
constituted an insurmountable barrier to the gang in their
attempts to seize power. For this reason, they tried to inspire
attacks on him and his memory....

The "gang of four's" past has been discussed and the
conduct of their members during the thirties has been investigated. This is not because it is in and of itself peculiar that each
committed different errors. A Marxist can never contend that
some person has always been right. This would be unreasonable. Whether it concerns a person in China or here in the
West, one can always find actions and views in the past—
articles and contributions, if it concerns people who write—
which are wrong and were incorrect already when they were
presented. This is not odd. The crucial question becomes, in

part, how a person relates to his past; whether or not he is prepared constantly to change and correct his ways. It becomes also a question of whether he acknowledges his past ways in general, which is itself a basic issue. China is a great country. The decades before Liberation were filled with momentous events. A person can cover up his tracks, as long as he can prevent others from going back to the files and documents.

The gang not only had committed errors and strange deeds during the thirties; they had also tried to cover them up. They tried to falsify history. It is in this area that their actions really became serious, indicating that their old ways had not been changed. The "gang of four" not only had a murky history; that history explained their wicked policies in the present. . . .

The gang's way of life upset people in China. On the one hand, they were real super-revolutionary apostles of clean living. On the other hand, its members lived very poshly and extravagantly, behaving like nouveaux riches. This hypocrisy reminds us in no small way of what we encounter among the leftslop in our own countries, those who complained that the European and American working classes have been bourgeoisified because workers have cars and TV sets and go on vacation.

The Chinese people have consciously settled accounts with drugs, prostitution and gambling. But this was not what the gang attacked. They campaigned against everyday interests and against the justifiable end-of-day relaxation of common workers, indiscriminately labeling people as reactionaries. They made politics something unbearably unpleasant. But the gang was a lot less critical of their own lifestyle.

They exploited their leading positions to order good and exclusive food and drink at restaurants and had the bill sent to the state; to procure automobiles for pleasure trips; and to get personal servants for themselves. Its members lived what could be called the Chinese equivalent of *la dolce vita,* which was completely in conflict with the Party's tradition. Chou En-lai, for instance, was always extremely careful to see that he did not exploit his great prestige and high post to personal advantage. To put it simply, Chou En-lai paid for himself when he ate at the Foreign Ministry's canteen. The gang neither ate at the canteen nor paid their own way. That angered people and was much talked about. Restaurant personnel saw how the members of the gang lived and did not keep quiet about it.

These are not, however, the main issues. If one makes them the main issues, then one turns reality upside down. In that case, it becomes Pekingology. But indeed these factors played a great role in the people's disgust for the "gang of four"....

In China, the struggle against the gang is now being conducted through extensive discussions. It is a question of weeding out their wrong line. But the Chinese are not striking against the many. Should each person who was out during the last year with slogans against the Party's line and who was taken in by the gang's line turn into an enemy? Are the youth who occupied the hotel in Chengtu and loudly fought the Party leadership in the summer of 1976 criminals to be put in prison? Of course not! As a clique, the "gang of four" has been crushed, and where there is a case of people who supported them, matters are being discussed....

Those so-called China-watchers, Pekingologists, make a basic mistake when they depict the events in China as a struggle between a few people at the top. It is not so, nor has it been so, save possibly at the university and publishing houses and organizations where the four had such influence that they succeeded in choking and restricting the policies and stifling all real debate. But in China as a whole, it was and is at the basic local level that things are happening. During the entire time I was there the discussions went on, continuing throughout the nights. Everywhere people sat together and talked, held meetings, and debated and discussed various questions. Party members held study meeting after study meeting, and the contradictions were intense. Now the discussions continue, and they are open and healthy, for the influence of the gang is in the process of completely dissipating. It is not a power struggle at the top. The debate in China concerns the question of which direction China will take. What is right? What is left? Through this discussion, the working class and all the people can attain unity and settle accounts with the false and dangerous line that the "gang of four" stood for.

Notes of an interview for
The Class Struggle
No. 96/1976 and No. 3/1977

Tsingtao residents learn of Mao Tsetung's death.

Students discuss the news.

Grief-stricken teachers

Remembering Chairman Mao

Workers carry funeral wreaths to the town's memorial hall.

At right, people line up for a memorial meeting.

Tsingtao's citizens pay final tribute to Mao Tsetung.

The people of Peking crowd the city's streets to attend a memorial meeting.

1977

Debate on the Left

The "Left's" Reaction

I wonder what the real nature of that which calls itself "left" in Europe and the United States is. Actually, I don't wonder, I think I know. But first, here is an example.

All the reports from China have described the "gang of four" as a small and isolated group with, at its height, a few million supporters (from among China's 900 million). All reports have described the politics of the four as being deeply unpopular in China.

I have not read of anyone in Europe or America seriously contending that Chiang Ching spoke for the Chinese working people. But this phony left, nonetheless, calls her radical and calls her and her friends' politics "left." And the newspapers of this trend mourn in their own way the decline and fall of the Chinese "left." The *Evening Sheet's* gossip column mourns reverently; the *Information* mourns intellec- tually; the Trotskyites in different countries mourn clamorous- ly; and such Marxist-Leninist organs as *Red Morning* in Germany seem to have gone into mourning silence after a final four-page homage to the gang. They all seem in agreement that there can be a left political line which opposes the people. With that, this European left stands exposed in all its nakedness for its real class character. People are completely correct in their distrust of them.

Let us examine the whole thing in a simple way. My political views are correct, I believe; but they are far from widespread in this society. Suppose that tomorrow I were given the power to realize my ideas. The power could be military (General Myrdal) or governmental power (Head of State Myrdal) or economic (Millionaire Myrdal). Journalists often pose such questions: If you got power, what would you do then?

The answer is simple. We all know it. In the best case, the attempts to realize my ideas would become meaningless gestures; in the worst, fascist terror.

For to *get* power means to get power over the people, and with such a power, no radical politics can be carried out. Such a power is always reactionary, even if it calls itself socialist as Hitler did, or revolutionary as Mussolini did, or communist as Brezhnev does, or nationalist as Pinochet does, or "left" as Chiang Ching did. The label doesn't change the power's character.

The people are the driving force in history. Revolutions which propel history forward are carried through by the great majority, precisely in the interests of the great majority. No people can be liberated from without; the working class's liberation must be through its own work.

Working in different ways for revolution, socialism and communism, and seeking to be left in the sense that we stand for the radical alternative, we partake in that liberation. Our work is necessary. But no one, not Robespierre, not Lenin nor Mao Tsetung, has ever fabricated a revolution!

The reactionaries are paper tigers. On September 20, 1792, the Prussian military machine, the most effective of its time, was beaten by the French volunteer army, a revolutionary people in arms. The Russian people in arms defeated their ostensibly superior enemy in the 1917-20 civil war; the Chinese people in arms were victorious, the Vietnamese people were also victorious through armed struggle. One can then pose the question to the great French revolutionaries, Lenin, Mao Tsetung or Ho Chi Minh: Who won? Who was the hero? And all those who were really leaders of great revolutions answer that it was the people. As Lenin said:

> It marks that great period when the dreams of liberty cherished by the best men and women of Russia *come true,* when liberty becomes the cause of the masses of the people, and not merely of individual heroes.*

The people are the driving force and constitute the great majority which fights for its own freedom. This is an elementary point for us in the radical and revolutionary tradition.

* V.I. Lenin, "A Contribution to the History of the Question of the Dictatorship," *Collected Works* (Moscow: Progress Publishers, 1966), vol. 31, p. 355.

This has nothing to do with occasional and shifting congressional majorities (although certainly congress can be used, but this is another question), nor does it have to do with aristocratic radicalism and fascistic petty bourgeois anarchism. Of course, it is necessary to have great leaders and they do exist, I have just named some, but it is the people who make history, and it is the people who are the heroes.

Now back to the European and American "left." It feels solidarity with Chiang Ching. It is itself elitist. It may itself play with the idea of revolution. This is why people are so distrustful of it. They see this "left" for what it is, a new ideological disguise of the middle layer which longs for elitist leadership.

Now suppose that you are standing one summer Sunday on the street. It is early in the morning and the street is deserted. Then three men come around the corner. They are coming toward you, walking abreast. Let us call them Smith, Sanchez and Jones. You see that Smith is walking on the left, and Jones on the right. You are standing there with newspapers. When they pass by, they wave decliningly at you, while they carry on their conversation, for they are on their way to church. You look after them then and they go on as before. But you see Jones on the left and Smith on the right.

Left and right thus change sides, and this does not say much about either Smith or Jones. They do not share your views, they say, while they are on their way to church that Sunday morning, as you sell newspapers. They do not buy a newspaper from you. But if you know that Jones works at GM and Smith is a service worker and Sanchez is a retired office worker on a pension; you also know that when it gets down to brass tacks, you belong to them and they to you, and the revolution cannot be made against them and the proletarian dictatorship cannot tyrannize them.

This is what Chiang Ching and the European and American "left" do not comprehend, and this is why most people do not want to have much to do with them.

The People in Pictures/Cultural Front
No. 1/1977

The Three Worlds as an Example

Indeed, there are heroes in world history. But they are of different sorts. Whether they are heroic or just great figures depends upon which side they are on. For us, the great figures of history are no heroes. For whom was Robert E. Lee a hero? For whom was Rommel a hero? And since we're not just talking about military figures, for whom was Nietzsche, Catherine the Second of Russia, Henry Ford or Golda Meir a hero? In any event, they're not ours.

But of course, we have our own heroes. Great people who have meant a lot for the liberation of mankind. Abraham Lincoln was such a hero. Engelbrekt was one in our own Swedish history. Dante Alighieri, Albert Einstein, Lu Hsun— they were all heroes on our side.

There are reasons for writing this. Hero worship is reactionary because all worship is paralyzing. But an incapacity to see greatness and draw lessons is also paralyzing. In his letter to Friedrich Sorge in March 1883, Frederick Engels wrote of Karl Marx who had passed away the day before:

> Mankind is shorter by a head, and the greatest head of our time. The movement of the proletariat goes on, but gone is the central point to which Frenchmen, Russians, Americans and Germans spontaneously turned at decisive moments to receive always that clear incontestable counsel which only genius and a perfect knowledge of the situation could give. Local lights and small talents, if not the humbugs, obtain a free hand. The final victory is certain, but the detours, the temporary and local errors— even now so unavoidable—will grow more than ever. Well, we must see it through; what else are we here for? And we are far from losing courage because of it.*

Mao Tsetung was one of the very greatest. For more than fifty years, he was a political leader with ever-growing

---

* Frederick Engels, "Engels to Sorge," *On Marx* (Peking: Foreign Languages Press, 1975), pp. 21-22.

responsibilities. As an aging person who was very well-read and had rich experience and a broad outlook of the world and of history, he retained a child's capacity to look at things with clear eyes filled with wonder. He was not a statesman who wrote poems in his leisure time. Rather, he was a statesman and a poet. He was therefore able as a politician, military leader and philosopher to make use of the possibilities of art to give vivid expression to the ever-shifting changes in conditions within China and the world.

His life was a long struggle, and as it was for Marx, so also for Mao Tsetung, that constant struggle was his real element. He pointed out that it was certainly not bad to be fought by one's enemies. But he was able to see that it was not necessarily good to be feted by those who claimed to be disciples.

His contributions to China's people were so great that everyone, including Chairman Mao himself, knew a generation ago that he had become an outstanding figure in modern China's history. He had indeed found a place in history. He was also sufficiently detached in a definite political situation— when the revolution hung in the balance and Liu Shao-chi tried to transform him into a political mummy—to make use of his actual historical authority to continue the revolution.

In front of all the statues, posters and paintings which represented him, Chairman Mao asked: "Shall I be handed down to posterity as a door god?" And when "the little red book" and "the three most commonly read" were spoken of, even when they were being used as a battering ram, he pointed out that it certainly did not hurt to read them; but it was a matter of reading what he had written in context, and of oneself taking a stand. He encouraged the reading of Marx, and serious reading at that.

In China, the reactionary forces could not before and cannot now propagate slogans hostile to Mao Tsetung and the revolution. Not even one percent, thus not even eight or nine million, would be able to unite around such slogans. This kind of situation has made for "red flags being fought by red flags" during the political struggle, which has gone on in China during recent decades. Mao Tsetung Thought can only be fought with "Maoism."

Lin Piao as well as the "gang of four" tried in this way to make use of Mao Tsetung's words and transform them into dogmas, phrases and ritual. It belongs to Mao Tsetung's greatness that he saw the hostile character of such tributes and fought against them. He never allowed his writings to become "Maoism."

Now he is dead. A mausoleum has been built in Peking, where he will rest in a memorial hall. Some people have wondered about this, feeling that this is some sort of cult. But this memorial hall represents no cult. It is being erected in accordance with the expressed wishes of the Chinese people. Millions upon millions of Chinese have in writings and resolutions to the Central Committee asked for a chance to express their grief and show their deep respect for him.

When Chou En-lai died, it became known that he had asked in his testament to be cremated and to have his ashes dispersed. His death was painful for the people, but these wishes of his made the pain more harsh, for they violated the customs of the Chinese people. People in Peking gathered and kept Chou En-lai's corpse from being taken to the crematorium. The workers at the crematorium then unanimously refused to carry out the cremation. It became necessary for the Premier's wife to ask that his wishes be respected and for Mao Tsetung to intervene, explaining that no one had a right to go against Comrade Chou En-lai's last wish. This was necessary so that the workers at the crematorium, with tears streaming down their cheeks, would carry out the behest.

Mao Tsetung has not yet been dead a year, and the struggle against his writings continues. Many European and American left intellectuals have for years imagined that those from Taiwan or people who are working with material from Taiwan, such as Stuart Schram, can discern what Mao Tsetung actually said. They are thus themselves capable of making revolution, or at least of producing scholarship. The KGB's disinformation experts are also participating in this game. To fight Mao Tsetung Thought, the KGB brass, the CIA and Taiwan are now being compelled to wave red flags and shout "Long Live." Here and there they are inspiring, setting up and subsidizing small "Maoist" groups who are playing with individual terrorism, kidnapping and a sort of "revolution," which has taken on terroristic and adventurous slogans. Naturally, this entire range of "Maoism," from academic Pekingology to provocative politics of petty assassinations, has nothing in common with Mao Tsetung Thought. But it has a lot to do with Lin Piao, the "gang of four," the KGB, the CIA and the Taiwan government.

To Mao Tsetung's greatness belongs his ability to clearly and simply express the necessary demands. From 1946 on, Mao Tsetung began developing the concept of the three worlds and pointed out that the third world is the main force in the struggle against imperialism, colonialism and hegemonism. He did so both on the basis of what Engels called "consummate knowledge of the situation," when he wrote about Marx, and with a deep familiarity with more than a century of Marxist discussion, as well as his own experiences in the struggle.

The third world is now the main force in the struggle against the hegemonism and imperialism of the two superpowers. We in Sweden are interested in uniting with the countries and peoples of the third world to oppose the superpowers and then, especially, the more predatory of the two, our neighbor, the Soviet Union. It is she who is now beginning to make territorial demands on us in the Baltic Sea. This is a view which corresponds to the experiences of the overwhelming majority of the Swedish people.

I am writing both that Mao Tsetung succeeded in formulating the necessary tasks and that this corresponds to our own experiences. I can take an example from my own experience. In 1958 I arrived for the first time in Asia. The experiences were presented in 1960 in the book *Crossroads of Cultures,* the first correct edition came out in 1971 under the title *Travel to Afghanistan.* The essential fact of this book is that it does not strive to "expose feudal oppression" in Afghanistan, but rather it takes a stand for Afghanistan against imperialism and tries to describe the long struggle against imperialism from the Kabul horizon.

The question of the third world is not new. What has happened is that the Soviet Union has developed into the most powerful and most predatory of the two superpowers, a country which now threatens us precisely like fascist Germany threatened us in 1937. We must therefore set up the broadest possible front for our defense.

Wonder not that the KGB, CIA and Taiwan are now waving red flags to oppose red flags!

The People in Pictures / Cultural Front
No. 6/1977

The Rationality of China's Foreign Policy

I.

It is not remarkable that on their own merits China's view of foreign policy and the positions she has taken on foreign policy are seen as incomprehensible or strange in Europe or America. China maintains that everything is pointing toward a great war in our time between the two superpowers; that the rhetoric of détente is part of the psychological warfare making Western Europe vulnerable, the way France became before 1940; that the point of contention is itself Europe, not Asia, Africa or Latin America. In short, for the third time in this century, eveything points to a world war on European soil.

China does not view both superpowers as equally desirous of war. It is now the Soviet Union which is the aggressive one, trying to expand and fight for a place in the sun, while the United States is seeking to keep what it has. The situation is not unlike the one which occurred some forty years ago when Hitler's Germany sought to wring an empire from the hands of

England. Since China has not only spoken of the threatening war in general, but also directly singled out the Soviet Union's preparations for war and has warned of her policies, it is not remarkable that the Soviet propaganda machine especially and its sub-entrepreneurs in various countries are seeking to present Mao Tsetung's view of war in our time as insane, immoral, reactionary and warmongering.

But this Chinese view of things also opens such an unpleasant perspective that many among us prefer to look away. We are repressing the insight. In China, they believe that this European and American repression of realities is in itself understandable. It corresponds to the conduct of Europe around 1912 or 1937. Now as then, this unwillingness to see reality contributes to making the coming war inevitable in a real sense, as well as longer, bloodier and more destructive.

But the question is not whether it was moral or immoral of Mao Tsetung (and therefore of his successors) to view the world in this way; nor is it one of whether it is reactionary or radical to foresee the coming war in Europe. Churchill was conservative. He never claimed to be anything else. He was also an imperialist and sought to preserve and strengthen the British Empire. Maxim Litvinov, Soviet representative to the League of Nations, was a communist. He was a Bolshevik and had world revolution as his aim.

Without renouncing their political convictions, they both reached the same judgment as to the deadly threat posed by Hitler's Germany. They viewed this threat as indeed a real one.

Churchill's and Litvinov's assertions that Hitler was arming for a great war were correct. We know this now, although it could already have been substantiated at the time. The question of whether it was a correct assertion or not could not be answered by referring to Churchill as a British imperialist or Litvinov as a Russian Jewish Bolshevik. But German propaganda tried to discredit their accurate description of the Nazi threat as a British imperialist and/or Russian Jewish invention. To a great extent, the German propaganda was successful. The correct description of the European situation was pushed aside into more or less extreme marginal newspapers while the mainstream press appeared sensible, it was said. The press in Europe did not become pro-Nazi in the thirties. It did not even become Nazi-influenced in general, but it succumbed to the pressures from Berlin in the sense that the press played a wait-and-see game and was not "unnecessarily provocative" by accepting Churchill's and Litvinov's apprehensions as a description of reality. Since these apprehensions were, however, well-founded, Hitler's arming and war policies were thereby facilitated.

Now Soviet propaganda is trying to portray every statement on the Soviet Union regarding its unprecedented arming for war as a Chinese "Maoist," German revanchist and/or American imperialist invention. And in the same way as forty years before, these statements are being confined to the outermost marginal newspapers while the leading mass media appears "sensible," without for that matter propagating the Kremlin's line. This signifies for the Soviet Union a great propaganda victory and, for Europe, the more imminent outbreak of war. For the assertion that the Soviet Union now, like Germany in 1937, is consciously preparing for a war of conquest through unprecedented armament is an assertion which can be investigated. Is it true or is it not that the Soviet Union is arming for war behind a curtain of phrases about peace?

Brezhnev's propagandists contend that every such question is warmongering, a breach of the spirit of Helsinki. From the Soviet Union's side (such as in UNESCO), it is demanded that the mass media in different countries should recognize their responsibility and strengthen peace by avoiding discussion of the Soviet Union's enormous arms expansion. On November 5, 1938, Adolf Hitler gave a speech at Weimar. He sought peace in Europe. He was of the opinion that a real disarmament also required a spiritual disarmament. Open slander and untruths about other countries were not allowed in Germany and in similarly disciplined countries. As Adolf Hitler could confirm, it was nevertheless different in the so-called democracies. There, types like Winston Churchill were allowed to insult Germany. But Adolf Hitler wanted to continue to work for the peace and security of Europe. There was only one condition however:

"The warmongers had to be disarmed." Brezhnev could not have said it better. (Nor does he say it better.) It's as if it had appeared in yesterday's *Pravda*.

At the same time that he spoke of peace at Weimar and accused the warmongers of lying about Germany, Hitler nevertheless armed for war. Plans were made for upcoming conquests and increased appropriations were given out of Germany's limited funds to the work of the fifth columns. The enormous Soviet armaments; the concentration on offensive weapons; the attempt to build up a fleet which will work on or under all seas; the offensive preparations at different bases; the continued military occupation of Czechoslovakia; the forced integration of vassal countries' military and economic resources; the ever-intensive Soviet spy activities in our countries and the repeated disinformation campaigns—all this is for real, completely irrespective of whether it is Chinese, Germans or Americans describing the conditions.

II.

For more than twenty years, since 1955 to be exact, the Soviet leadership has conducted a war of propaganda against China. This was done first internally, then on the party level to all parties and groups outside the country which they had control over or influence on, and gradually in a completely open manner. Now, after twenty years, it is being conducted through every conceivable channel.

One thrust of this propaganda war consists of planned disinformation regarding events in China. The Soviet specialists of disinformation and news wire warfare have begun to take over the leading role which propagandists of the American China lobby played in the fifties and sixties, when their aim was to distort the picture of Chinese development.

Now the Kremlin is working hand-in-glove with Taipei to continue this sordid telegram service.

The Soviet state leadership has a direct interest in Europe's people getting the notion that China's economic problems are insoluble, that China is on the verge of a civil war, and that all politics in China are an expression of palace intrigue between different groups and people in the quarters surrounding the Forbidden City of Peking.

This Soviet propaganda against China sometimes works with direct lies. But above all and most effectively, it works with distortion. China does have economic problems. She is a country of the third world which is trying by her own efforts to rise out of misery. So these problems are presented as insurmountable. Because China is not monolithic, she is presented as verging on the brink of civil war. Even if by tradition Chinese society is closed to foreigners, the political contradictions in China appear in a very open way and are described in political terms. So China is described as falling apart. Different people in China have represented different political lines. So the social struggle among China's 800 or 900 million is presented as a result of private agreements between different individuals.

As especially indicative of China's dissolution, the Soviet propagandists present "interpretations" of her social life. Among their observations, these propagandists point to wall newspapers that appear to contradict each other; the fact that politicians who have been wildly attacked in certain wall posters are later not removed from their positions; and that politicians, who are the objects of serious criticism and have disappeared, turn out to be alive, can again receive trusted tasks and assume leading positions. I find it remarkable that this Soviet indignation, so strongly characteristic of their own monolithic state traditions from the czars' time, finds a limited response in Europe.

It is of course not good that the picture of China is distorted. But the Soviet propaganda war against China has not been expanded to its present extent because the Soviet regime has an ideological conflict with China. Neither is this extensive propaganda war even a consequence of the border disputes between the two countries nor of the armed conflicts which have taken place at the Ussuri or up in Sinkiang. The issue of borders would actually be very easy to solve. All that is really required is that the present Soviet regime be prepared to follow the agreement between the Soviet Union and China of May 31, 1924, and that she agree to respect the boundaries which Article VII of this agreement stipulated, but which were never carried out. Just as the ideological issues, which the Soviet regime raises to camouflage itself, are only rationalizations; so the Soviet intransigence on the border issue is only an expression of the really serious contradiction with China, which has driven the Soviet regime to allocate ever greater resources to an international disinformation campaign. It is this which makes it a serious problem for us in Europe and America so that our picture of China is distorted.

It can be put this way: Mao Tsetung's articulation of the three worlds theory in 1974 explains the Soviet leaders' determination in their campaign against China. That this observation then appears in Europe or America as an unreasonable assertion is really only proof of how successful this Soviet campaign has been. I am quite sure that most do not know what Mao had to say on the three worlds, and few of the politicians and writers who read about the three worlds then understood what it was he was actually pointing out.

Since this question is extremely important, let me quote the statement of China's United Nation's delegation in a speech on October 5, 1976, to the UN's General Assembly. The speech was presented by the foreign minister of that time, Chiao Kuan-hua. He has since then vacated his post; but the speech itself was not a personal one, rather a governmental declaration which is still valid:

> Making a penetrating analysis of all the basic contradictions of our time and the division and realignment of all the political forces in the world, Chairman Mao Tsetung advanced his great strategic concept of the three worlds.

> He pointed out: The United States and the Soviet Union make up the first world; the developing countries in Asia, Africa, Latin America and elsewhere constitute the third world; and in between the two is the second world composed of Europe, Japan, Canada and other countries. Lenin once said: Imperialism is the progressing oppression of the nations of the world by a handful of great powers; it is an epoch of wars among these powers for the extension and consolidation of national oppression. At present, the Soviet Union and the United States, the two superpowers constituting the first world, are the biggest international oppressors and exploiters of our time and they are the sources of a new world war. While the developed countries of the second world oppress and exploit third world countries, they themselves are at the same time subjected to superpower oppression, exploitation, control or threat. The numerous third world countries are most heavily oppressed and exploited by colonialism and imperialism; they are the main force in the fight against imperialism, and particularly against superpower hegemonism.*

To get a correct perspective on what Mao Tsetung is saying here, we should think back over the last 500 years of history. Then the present reckless rage against China by the Soviet leaders would also become comprehensible.

At the end of the fifteenth century, culturally advanced countries were found in all parts of the world, including Africa and America. They all were in a state of social and economic development, change and transformation. (The historical view that stagnation existed outside Europe is a myth, and a myth which has legitimized colonialism.) Whoever wants to search for a truly developed society could do so in what is now the third world: in the Ming Dynasty's China or maybe in the Delhi's Sultanate. In any case, not in the outlying Russian and North American regions. The disparate development made it

* Chiao Kuan-hua, "The Chinese Government Will Continue to Carry Out Resolutely Chairman Mao's Revolutionary Line and Policies in Foreign Affairs," *Peking Review,* No. 42, Oct. 15, 1976, pp. 12-13.

possible, however, for the European world to conquer great portions of the world. But these 500 years of colonialism, when European countries like Spain and Britain set up empires and sought world domination, represent an epoch which already belongs to the past.

The third world is liberating itself; it is regaining its place the world is again becoming multifarious. In a longer range perspective, these 500 years are only a short hour of imbalance. In this case, it means not only that the era of European world empires has passed, but also that colonial-type empires have become outdated. If the third world's liberation can be realized, then there will not be universal monarchy. The Soviet leaders' dreams of a worldwide "socialist community" under the Kremlin will become a short-lived eternity like Hitler's thousand-year reich or the American Century.

It was during the thirties that Mao Tsetung began working out the analysis which culminated in the concept of the three worlds in 1974. The basic lines are found in his articles and speeches of that time. The conversations with Edgar Snow also made clear the difference between Moscow's view of China's conditions and the politics Mao Tsetung recommended.

At that time, Mao Tsetung believed the Soviet Union's general politics were in the main correct. He would later formulate it that Stalin was seventy percent correct and thirty percent incorrect in his policies. By not following the directions of Moscow after World War II, Mao Tsetung was able to lead his forces to victory in the civil war against the Kuomintang and to initiate the work of raising China out of misery and destruction.

To this day, the Chinese still admire Stalin for recognizing his mistakes. During two months of very hard negotiations which Mao Tsetung spent in Moscow and which ended in a treaty between China and the Soviet Union being signed on February 14, 1950, Stalin acknowledged before the Chinese representatives that he had been wrong. When China's ambassador to Moscow held a reception at the adoption of the treaty at Hotel Metropol in Moscow, Stalin attended. It was the first time in twenty-seven years that he had been guest at a dinner   party in Moscow outside the Kremlin walls. He did not come in uniform, but wore civilian clothes, and he took the occasion to ask Mao Tsetung to accept his apology for the errors and mistakes he had committed in relation to China. He was, as the Chinese say, not only very hard in negotiations, but also was prepared to recognize the actual conditions and to waive an implicit Soviet suzerainty over China. Mao Tsetung was singularly prepared, for China's part, to enter into cooperation on equal terms. Stalin accepted this.

When the international polemic within the communist world movement of the day became public in the early sixties and the French communist leader Maurice Thorez attacked China, the Chinese answered by pointing out that, among other things, Thorez had not extended his support to the oppressed and colonized peoples' wars of liberation. Indeed, the people of Algeria were also obliged to fight for their liberation against the leadership of the French Communist Party. What was at the time said by China was that this conduct showed that European communists like Thorez had long abandoned Lenin's understanding of the oppressed people's liberation and had gone over to the imperialist camp in opposition to the third world. It was also pointed out by the Chinese side that those like Thorez betrayed the foremost duty of communists, serving the people. They found themselves in a circumstance of fawning subservience to foreign overlords. This is why they proved themselves incapable of serving the French people's interests at a crucial moment.

In his conversation with Anna Louise Strong in 1946, Mao Tsetung had presented his view of world politics. On some important points, it differed from those views beginning to be characteristic of Moscow as, clearly recalling this conversation, *Pravda* rancorously pointed out in 1964. This view later led to Mao Tsetung's efforts at contacting politicians like de Gaulle and trying to extend ties to powers such as Japan and the German Democratic Republic. In *Pravda's* furious attack on Mao Tsetung on September 2, 1964, they formulated what

was later to become the pseudo-left's patented argument
against China:

> This theory already saw the light of day in 1946. In its
> original form, it was as follows: the Chinese leaders
> divide the globe into three parts, or zones. Exactly like
> the poet who put horses and people in a jumble all
> together, Chairman Mao has mixed together exploiter
> and exploited, oppressor and oppressed in the interme-
> diate zone. In the conversation [Mao Tsetung's Conver-
> sation with Japanese socialists—J.M.] it was said: "All
> the people of Asia, Africa and Latin America are coming
> out against imperialism, and Europe, Canada and other
> countries are also coming out against imperialism."
> Notice that it is not the working people in Europe and
> Canada but precisely all of Europe and all of Canada,
> including the capitalist monopolies, the reactionary
> bourgeois parties, the French "ultras," the revanchists in
> Bonn, etc. . . . This is why they (Chinese leaders) made the
> first intermediate zone out of Asia's, Africa's and Latin
> America's countries, including China. Since the Chinese
> leaders are furthermore looking for rich economic part-
> ners and potential allies in the international arena among
> developed capitalist countries, they include almost the
> entire capitalist world in the intermediate zone and give it
> a mandate as champion against imperialism.

I am citing *Pravda* for three reasons. In part, it can be of interest to see who formulated the arguments against China
which are now floating about in the more general European
left and which are mainly spread in Sweden by *The Evening
Sheet*. In part, I cite it because 1964 is a good intermediate
point. At that time the current world picture was being shaped,
even if the United States still stood out as the most powerful
superpower state, in a class by itself, as the superpower. But,
most importantly, precisely because *Pravda's* hostile account
of Mao Tsetung's view makes it easier to answer the question
of whether or not he was right.

The interesting thing about Mao Tsetung's view and what makes his summary of 1974 of the three worlds so important for us is really what has brought about the last decade's enormous escalation of Soviet propaganda warfare against China. That is to say, his conception is demonstrably correct. And, in the long run, it will also become a guiding star for the politics of the world. Irrespective of what those who participate in politics think of the Chinese or of communists, this will be so.

The first world consists of the superpowers. The Soviet Union and the United States are superpowers. We can discuss their relative balance of power, we can discuss their different political and military judgments, but there is no doubt they are in direct rivalry and regard each other as the main enemy. They themselves say, and their henchmen with them, that each is fighting to deter the other from world domination. This is a less offensive way of saying that they find themselves in contention for world hegemony. This contention will sooner or later lead to a military showdown. It is a matter of fact that it is not only the Chinese who believe that superpower rivalry and the arms spiral has now passed the point of no return, the point from which war has become inevitable; that the Soviet Union has now become the driving and aggressive force in this rivalry and that the United States, especially after its defeat in Vietnam, now finds itself on the defensive.

That the third world's liberation is one of the great events of our time should be clear to all. There is not just a difference on the map between 1937 and 1977; there is also a difference in quality of the political forces. Naturally, this is a long and sometimes contradiction-filled process, but the balance of the world is being reestablished after 500 years. The third world is poor, having been suppressed and exploited, "underveloped" it is called.

The question is what is characteristic of the third world. A gloomy picture can be painted of poverty, oppression and misery. The Swedish mass media's picture of India is, for instance, like this. Especially some who are calling themselves left in Europe and America are painting a gloomy picture of the third world too; the big enemies here in the world are thought to be the Latin American generals, African presidents, the Shah of Iran, Indian profiteers and police in Sri Lanka. This is a picture which is sometimes not infrequently called anti-imperialist and replete with solidarity.

In the Swedish media in general and from the phony left in particular, China is usually accused of betrayal to the cause, because the people there are not participating in this gloomy depiction. China is said to have a bourgeois view of Asia, unlike the European left's own revolutionary view of it. It is true that, for instance, the portrayal of India prevalent on Swedish television and in the Swedish press is not the same as China's, not even when Chinese and Indian troops stood face to face in armed conflict.

There have, however, also been groups in China who have wanted to portray the third world the way it is depicted by the European pseudo-left. It was the same groups who burnt the British buildings in Peking and who are regarded in China as a provocative extreme right in left disguise.

I think I know which of these two pictures is the correct one. For almost twenty years, I have travelled and worked in the third world. I have tried to describe these countries as honorably as I was able. But aside from one blunder in 1959, when I got caught up in the enthusiasm of my Afghan friends for Pashtunistan and made an incorrect attack on Pakistan (which I deleted in subsequent editions of the Afghan book), my description fits in better with the Chinese view than with what usually calls itself the European left's solidarity movement. But my view of Afghanistan or India has not been shaped by China. It was actually the other way around: my experiences in Iran, Afghanistan, India and other countries gave me a view of the third world which made it possible for me to later describe China.

In spite of all difficulties, contradictions and momentary setbacks, the third world is in forward movement and the 500 year interlude is over.

China is a country in the third world. But it is not just a developing country; it is a country in genuine development. This was true even during the most difficult years, when plans went awry, when there was also crop failure and the Soviet regime opportunely used foreign assistance as blackmail, abrogated contracts, summoned home the Soviet experts and had them take with them blueprints and reserve parts. Even during these dark years when the Chinese people really suffered heavily, China succeeded in continuing its construction through its own efforts. China is a great example of the potential of the third world. And China is no small enclave with a few million inhabitants but, rather, an enormous expanse with enormous problems.

It is the third world's rise which is inevitably disintegrating every plan for world domination. And in spite of all difficulties, in spite of the picture of confusion and misery which is being communicated through our mass media (a picture which fills an appropriate function for the superpowers), the third world's recouping of its rightful place in the world is an inevitable and irreversible process.

This process could not even be stopped if China changed and became a mini-superpower, an aggressive power in Asia. Such a development is naturally conceivable. Many times during the past decades, it could have been thought that China was about to go this route. It is not without reason that China's neighbors therefore experienced with relief Lin Piao's descent as well as the struggle against the "gang of four." In a limited way and for a limited time such a development in China would have only been able to stop or delay the rise of the third world. A Chinese Asia would be as unrealistic a vision as an American Century or a worldwide "socialist community" directed by the Kremlin.

As for the second world, it is evident that Mao Tsetung's description is correct. Portugal, Spain and Great Britain have given up every pretension to world domination. France, Holland and Belgium have ended their colonial rule. Japan, Germany and Italy, countries which a generation ago participated in the contention for world domination, have not only lost a round, they have pulled out of the game completely. Much can be said about the mentality of authority in the German Federal Republic. Economically it is a more powerful state than Hitler's Germany, but it would be completely unreasonable to assert that the German Federal Republic was seeking world domination or hegemony.

In his judgment of the different forces in Europe as well, Mao Tsetung showed he was right.... It was not French socialists and/or Thorez who were capable of protecting the interests of the French people during the war in Algeria. It was de Gaulle who brought an end to the opposition of reactionary colonialists, fascist-like superiors and influential holdouts. He made peace with Algeria and set North Africa loose. This was a principled and correct policy which served the people of both France and Algeria, a patriotic policy in the good sense. Thorez and the socialists had had their special tie with the superpowers and had, therefore, become incapable of serving the interests of the French people.

The contradictions between the second world and the third world are known. It is no secret that a hard tug-of-war for raw materials' prices and industrial goods' prices, among other things, is going on. At the same time, it is exactly what *Pravda* suspected in 1964: they are in need of each other and have common interests against the superpowers.

Had Mao Tsetung's analysis of the three worlds not been simultaneously so correct and so easy to comprehend, the Soviet regime would not have needed to make such enormous efforts to spread misinformation about it and about China.

III

China is following world political events with great attention. Her information about foreign affairs is extensive and varied. Abroad, the extent as well as the diversity are often underestimated. It can be put this way: the average Chinese reader has significantly better general knowledge of the world than, for example, the average reader in the German Federal

Republic. It is not possible to compare this with the regimentation in the Soviet Union and its satellite countries.

The reason why foreigners often underestimate the diversity of Chinese foreign information is usually that they only consider what is in the *People's Daily* or what is supplied by the news agency, New China. There, the news material is very carefully sifted. Especially during the years when the "gang of four" controlled the mass media, it was often rather one-track. But this is not the only available information on foreign affairs in China. The newspaper *Reference News* contains telegrams from foreign agencies which are not commented on, as well as translations of articles from the foreign press, and it maintains a pretty high standard.

Whoever reads the *People's Daily* as well as the *Reference News* gets a perspective which is very broad. It can be said that this perspective corresponds approximately to the one European readers of *Le Monde* can get.

The *Reference News* is not an unedited newspaper. There is no such thing. But its aim is to accurately report world political events and and foreign commentaries and positions. Such information was once available only to a few. Chou En-lai sought to break down such barriers; the "gang of four" sought to preserve them. For the last few years, the *Reference News* has been almost completely public. It is, however, not yet sold freely. Foreigners cannot buy it. I have seen it read by shop assistants in Tsingtao, workers in Lanchow, workmen in I-li and installation workers in Taklamakan. The Chinese public is significantly better informed about world politics than is generally assumed in Europe.

China is not screened off from the discussions being conducted outside the country's borders. All overseas Chinese have the right to travel freely to China and they are *guaranteed* the right to leave. One runs into these overseas Chinese throughout China. Taiwan is a part of China, and the Kuomintang still reigns there. But all the people in Taiwan have the right to travel freely to the mainland and are also guaranteed the right to travel back home. This is a general right irrespective of political conviction. There are also small transistor radios for sale everywhere at a very low price, and anyone who wants to can listen to foreign broadcasts over them.

Working conditions for foreign journalists are difficult. There are different reasons for this, and there are also traditional reasons for this. But one should not draw the conclusion from this that China is closed and cut off. The fall of the "gang of four" will certainly lead to a significant increase in mutual exchange and mutual contacts between China and other countries. In other words, the carrying out of Chou En-lai's policies.

Chinese foreign policy was formulated by Mao Tsetung. It was worked out by Chou En-lai and was affirmed in the documents of different programs accepted by the decision-making organs of the country. There is a strong popular support for this policy, but it is important to keep in mind that this support is not completely shaped by a controlled propaganda. It is not like the opinion shaped in the Soviet Union or shaped in Hitler's Germany, which melted away every time the citizens happened to tune into an "enemy radio station" on their receivers or happened to read prohibited views in print.

There is no reason to depict China as a liberal country. That it is not, nor has it ever been. But the popular support for China's foreign policies is a well-considered one in the proper sense of the word. For conceptions which are regarded as really incorrect and dangerous are carefully studied "to learn by negative example." So, for example, the Soviet leaders' arguments against Mao Tsetung and against China are known in more detail in the Chinese countryside than in the somewhat intellectually active Soviet cities.

IV

It is often said that China is interested in increased tension in Europe to divert the Soviet Union's pressure from her own border. China wants conflict in Europe to protect herself. It is believed in China that this is an incorrect understanding.

Around 1969 there was speculation in many areas that a war between the Soviet Union and China would arise. The invasion of Czechoslovakia and the Soviet Union's military occupation of the country, which was silently accepted by the other powers, together with the doctrine of the socialist countries' limited sovereignty formulated by Brezhnev, was believed to be paving the way for a Soviet attack on China, maybe to "reestablish the socialist order." It was believed that the Soviet border attacks and the different provocations were intended to create direct pretexts for such an attack. In the world press, Soviet military preparations on China's borders were written about.

But the Soviet probes at the border showed China's preparedness was good. If the Soviet leaders thought China would fall like ripe fruit as soon as they pulled across the borders, they were forced to reconsider. Abroad and in Taiwan, the press spoke of the Soviet threat as imminent; but in China, the leadership made a strategic analysis of the situation. A comprehensive Soviet attack on China was not feasible. The Soviet Union's main enemy was and remained the United States. Under these circumstances, the Soviet leadership had to reckon with the fact that if it attacked China militarily, it could lose Moscow before its forces had reached Peking.

Had the situation been different and China's preparedness been poor, had the country been deeply divided and persons who were prepared to serve as agents for the Kremlin seized power within the central leadership, the Soviet Union would have then been able to fulfill the czars' old dreams of incorporating northwest China (Sinkiang) and northeast China (formerly called Manchuria) and keeping the rest as a dependent servile country. In his desperate plan for a coup d'état, Lin Piao also toyed with similar thoughts.

To counter these schemes, as Mao Tsetung had contended, it was necessary to increase preparedness and see to it that China's foreign policy did not fall into the rut of seeking supremacy. Chinese preparedness is built upon the people's conscious will and ability to defend the country. But it was a misunderstanding to believe, as some youth did, that it sufficed to have revolutionary enthusiasm. Anti-aircraft defenses were needed; and it wouldn't hurt to have tanks, considering it was a matter of keeping the Soviet leaders' armed forces on the right side of the border.

A real Soviet attempt to subdue China was to be reckoned with. This would happen at the point when the Soviet Union won sovereignty over Western Europe (through open war or through a protracted process of Finlandization), seized power over West Asia, and given the United States a decisive defeat, which would at least have forced it to withdraw beyond the oceans.

If the European states hope to achieve security by letting the Kremlin go against the East, the result for Europe will be as catastrophic as Chamberlain's and Daladier's policies.

The leaders of the Soviet Union wish to achieve control over the highly industrialized Western Europe. The fact that they are arming their forces for this conquest with credit from the prospective victims is one of history's ironies. The argument that the leaders in the Kremlin would abstain from war in Europe because it would risk destroying the Western European industries they are out to get does not hold up. Experience shows that material destruction in a highly industrialized and organized country is only able temporarily to hinder the expansion of the productive apparatus. Germany's industry during and after World War II is a good example of this. Under the logic of imperialism, material devastation becomes a reasonable price to pay to get Western Europe.

But it is felt in China that the United States has much too great an interest in Western Europe to simply withdraw without much ado. It is in Western Europe that a Soviet challenge is leading to world war. There is ample but not overwhelming reason to believe that the United States would view an attack on Western Europe as an attack on its own most vital interests. The Western European countries cannot put their trust in the United States. It is possible that the United State would give up and withdraw into isolationism. The only ones who can protect Western Europe are the people of Western Europe.

Ultimately, in every war, it is the people who are decisive. To say it is the people's defense which is decisive and that, for instance, Yugoslavia's concentration on popular defense is good, does not mean that Western Europe need not defend itself with weaponry. But it is the preparedness of the people which will become decisive in the end.

The fact that the Chinese speak of a coming war and discuss self-defense against attack does not mean they are contending that war is good or war is desirable. It is also clear in the long run that the Kremlin certainly can begin a war, but the imperialists can never achieve their dreamed-of goal. They will never have world hegemony. The Soviet rockets will face the same fate as the Spanish Armada. It is like Mao Tsetung said, all reactionaries are in the long run paper tigers; but, as he also pointed out, here and now they are the real tigers with real claws. Imperialists have their own logic and all their words of détente, disarmament and test-bans are only idle talk. Their actions refute their words by the minute. Neither of the two superpowers will attain hegemony. In the long run, it will be the countries of the third world, who today are on the rise, that will reestablish the world balance. There will be new contradictions which will push their development forward beyond hegemony and wars. But even if we were to view the contention of the Soviet Union and the United States for world domination with the same detachment that we have in observing the contention between Spain and England and the fate of the Spanish Armada, still, we do live in the here and now. It is we who shape history within the framework of possibilities.

If the imperialists such as today's overlords in the Kremlin were receptive to common sense and reason, people would not have to suffer from wars and oppression. But they follow their own logic. This is why war in Europe is inevitable. That it cannot thus be avoided does not mean that it cannot be delayed; war can be put off and just the measures needed to delay the war signify that the coming war can be won with less sacrifice. Greater preparedness, popular defense and cooperation between those countries now threatened by the leaders in the Kremlin all serve to delay the war and make it possible to win with less sacrifice.

A policy of appeasement, such as Chamberlain and others pursued prior to the last great war, guarantees that war will come sooner. It means it will be more destructive and reap more victims.

The governments of the Eastern European countries, with the exception of Yugoslavia and Romania, are not independent governments. They are client states which have to act according to orders. But the people in those countries, and even the people in the Soviet Union, want to determine their own destiny and do not want to be controlled by the KGB and live under occupation of the Kremlin's military forces. Their struggle for freedom is difficult. But it is a correct and just struggle for national liberation. The situation in Europe reminds us therefore of the one existing in the years before World War II. Only a broad alignment of forces which can stand against aggression will succeed in withstanding them.

We should however pay attention to the fact that Brezhnev, like the old czars before him and like Hitler in his time, is trying to take advantage of those national liberation movements over which they gain control. This is the way the czars worked under the guise of pan-slavism, and the way the Japanese tried to make use of the Indian people's heroic freedom struggle. But those who believed they could avail themselves of the czars or of the Japanese militarists to gain their freedom had a rude awakening. This should be kept in mind now, when Brezhnev is making a go of it with the same methods.

It so happened that personal friends in China, whom I had known many years, were discussing Sweden. They were not official spokesmen and we were talking on a personal level, like old friends. They had been well acquainted with Swedish affairs over many decades and there were a few questions they were curious about.

How could it actually happen that Olof Palme [Swedish prime minister of early seventies—ed.] never visited China? Could it have been Russian pressure which led to Palme's never visiting there and never having the occasion to speak with Mao Tsetung and Chou En-lai?

A much more serious conjecturing came from one who follows Sweden's policy from a distance, but not in practice: Does Sweden really contemplate defending herself? In all cases? Even if the United States does not come to her aid?

It was uncomfortable for me not to be able to give a clear and firm answer to their questions. But behind this lay the uncertainty of whether Sweden is being Finlandized and quietly gliding under the shadow of the Kremlin.

Swedish Daily
3/20, 3/22, 3/24/1977

China's Image Abroad

Many readers believe that in some significant way China's political course has changed during the last years. The course of 1977 is supposedly no longer the course of 1975. Between them lies the 1976 settlement with the "gang of four." It is unfortunate that they believe so, since this view is incorrect.

The political decisions which fixed the course of development were made by the Tenth Party Congress and the Fourth National People's Congress, and they were in effect in 1975, as in 1976 and 1977. However, a struggle has been conducted. The struggle is not being conducted in the forms of congressional or parliamentary democracy. But it is this political and social struggle among China's hundreds of millions which is the really determining factor. China is not monolithic, and the Chinese debate very concrete issues. The struggle is wholly comprehensible to everyone.

But the Swedish public has been poorly informed about this. In leading newspapers such as the *Daily News,* the public has not been able to read news about Peking or to know exactly what is said in Peking, for the *Daily News'* coverage has become irregular and private. About China, the *Daily News* "feels" and "knows" and "wonders." The information follows afterward.

There is also a current European-American phenomenon contributing to distorting the picture of China. It is the "disappointed left."

In the wake of the student protests, youth revolts and the sixties struggle against the war in Vietnam, many young graduates left the universities. Now, in the seventies, there is no longer an economic boom. Now there is mass unemployment and the wind is blowing cold. Now this new left is being winnowed. The chaff is blowing away with the wind.

Now it is coming to light that large groups of that left had selected China as their private utopia. China became the country where no mother struck her child; where all drug addicts were treated with love and understanding. Yes, China was considered one single and protracted mass meeting.

The picture was wrong. When the reality did not coincide with their notions, those European and American left-intellectuals "corrected" the reality in China so that it would coincide with European student-left views.

So, for instance, Claudine Broyelle wrote in *Women's Liberation in China,** an excellent book which, unfortunately, is unreliable on a few central issues. In *Berlin Notebooks No. 4, 1977,* she describes her journalistic method:

> When we visited the small street factories, the Chinese women who received us always said: "Thanks to the Party, in 1958 we could do this or that...." In spite of this, I decided to write nothing about the Party but rather to say the following: "In 1958, the women decided...."

* Claudine Broyelle, *Women's Liberation in China* (Atlantic Highlands, New Jersey: Humanities Press, Inc., 1977).

> By saying it was the women's own initiative, I showed the
> power of the masses. I showed the democracy at the local
> level and could avoid the problem with the Party.*

Now, Claudine Broyelle is disappointed with China. The
Party is there, the state is there and authority is there. But it
was indeed not the Chinese who fooled her.

Any normal professional small town journalist would have
done better work. For there being a party and a state and
authority in China can only become an astonishing disappointment for a student politician without contact with the real
world.

It was China's misfortune that for a while this type of
European and American left dreamed a China. Now, in the icy
blast of the seventies, the members of that left are displaying
signs of disappointment with China in order to escape the cold
and to take up their careers again.

But it is not China's fault, and it is not China which has
changed.

The picture of China is also distorted in another way. In
connection with Mao Tsetung's death and the "gang of four's"
fall, the propaganda campaign against China, pushed for a
long time by clear political motives from Moscow and Taipei,
was escalated into a massive disinformation campaign.

On two counts, the campaign has been very successful. It
has succeeded in establishing the notion in many readers that
the Cultural Revolution has now been wholly negated, that
China has become "reactionary." It has also succeeded, in
general, in hindering the general public in our countries from
becoming conscious that China believes itself to have fully
rational grounds to see a third world war as inevitable. And
it has succeeded in hindering the discussion of these grounds
and the fact that if they are valid, they are valid irrespective of
whether you are a rightist or social democrat, pacifist, Chris-
tian, liberal or communist.

What contributed to the success of the disinformers from

* Cite not available in English.

Moscow was that rather large groups in Europe and America are now, in this pre-war period, engaging in a flight from reality of the same sort as during the 1930 decade of Hollywood make-believe films, sexual liberation and psychologizing.

It is necessary to reason coldly and sensibly about the coming war, and only insight into what is happening now can help the people prepare themselves so as to be able to live through the coming decade with a minimum of mass death and destruction. When China puts this forward she is then set upon with raving accusations of warmongering. It is explicable but lamentable for all of us....

The Express
7/3/77

Twenty-fifth Anniversary of the Swedish-Chinese Friendship Federation

On the occasion of its twenty-fifth anniversary, the Swedish-Chinese Friendship Federation is now taking a new great step forward in its work. It is developing from a federation into a popular movement and thus faces new, ever greater and ever more demanding tasks and responsibilities.

This is not just an internal organizational issue. The Federation does not exist for its own sake. When the organization was founded in 1952, it was composed of a small group of thirty people. It grew from an association in Stockholm into an association with branches all over the country. It then developed into a nationwide federation. Now the Federation is on its way to becoming a popular movement. As such, with 10,000 members, we are still one of the smaller movements, but we are now striving for a membership of 50,000. The tasks and responsibilities are increasing all the time. This development is an expression of the Swedes' ever more conscious desire for friendship and increased mutual exchange with China.

It is not as if we had created the Swedish people's friendship for the people of China. We are an expression of this genuine friendship. But if we do our work poorly, we may do harm to this friendship. If we assume our responsibility and do our work correctly, we will promote friendship. The Swedish people's friendship for China's people and their ever increasing understanding of and respect for China will exist irrespective of whether we are around or not. It is this genuine friendship which has created and developed us and for which our organization is an expression. By carrying out our work poorly, we may harm it, and by doing our work well, we will be able to contribute to its development. But it is not we who have created this friendship. It is this friendship which has created us.

Sometimes the work we do to promote friendship may consist of great gala celebrations. But most of it consists of everyday tasks. All over the country many people are at work to develop understanding and mutual exchange between Sweden and China. Of what does this work consist? It is running off stencils, committee meetings, arranging meetings in schools and libraries. It consists of lectures and talks, the showing of slides and film-strips, and discussions. It is work done under our own management and also that done by our members in the trade unions and political and other organizations. Not the least, it consists of discussions at work and in canteens.

This work is the foundation. Without this work, there is no organized friendship. For what is the good of a gala celebration like this one to the Swedish people's understanding of China if the issues are not discussed properly by people in factories, schools and offices? Both this celebration and the extensive discussion in thousands of work places express friendship work. They are both necessary, and they are each other's precondition.

The everyday work sustaining the friendship work is not work for today and tomorrow and the day after tomorrow. It is *long-term* work. Enthusiasm is itself an excellent thing. But it is, as a young woman once said to her suitor, "Love me a little but love me for a long time."

We have no great need of people who flare up like dry straw in love for China and who then quickly burn down and turn to ashes. Such people do exist. Experience in friendship work during the past shows that exactly those who most vehemently accuse the rest of us of being half-hearted and weak in our feelings towards China and not sufficiently ardent and who are 210 percent friends of China...will the next year be as disappointed in China as strongly as they were in love with China before. One year they charge us with half-heartedness, the next year they charge us with eternally opportunistic faithfulness to China.

But the work we do to promote friendship is patient *long-term* work. It is not a matter of sudden and violent passion for China but of an organized expression of the Swedish people's need of and desire for mutual understanding and mutual exchange between Sweden and China. Thus, the work is not only long-term, but important and responsible as well.

We often point out that this friendship work is not a privilege of one or the other group. Outside friendship work, we as an organization have no comprehensive political or social purposes. We take a stand concerning different public issues only to the extent that they affect the relations between our two peoples, our two states. That is of course correct. It is also important that it be said.

Here in the Friendship Federation, Conservative Party people, Liberal Party people, Center Party people, social-democrats, communists and non-partisan affiliated people work together. Some of our members are active in a political party on the local, county or national level. To a certain extent, the issue of what government Sweden is to have is decided by the different work of our different members; but, as an organization, we do not take a stand on this issue. Our task is to work for friendly relations and increased exchange. But that does not mean that we as an organization demand some kind of political sexlessness from our members, be they active or not. On the contrary, we regard it as a strength that friendship work is rooted in the different layers of political activists. This shows that friendship between Sweden and China is not of a temporary or party-tactical character.

Many different outlooks are represented in the Swedish-Chinese Friendship Federation. We have religious members and we have members who are indifferent to religious matters or atheists. But in our Federation, we work together. People from different classes and social backgrounds also participate here too. Not only do we have corporate directors and retail workers as members, but we also have members of the Swedish Employers' Association and members of the Swedish Confederation of Trade Unions in the organization. We have more members from the latter than from the former... but, then, there are many more of the latter.

We can say that we have people both from high positions and from the general mainstream. Representatives from those in leading positions of industry, politics, public administration, trade unions, academic life, the press and the arts, as well as of the broad masses of the people. We can also say that the more we develop in the direction of a popular movement, the more evident this feature of our Federation will be. As we grow from an association into a federation, and from a federation into a popular movement, our profile, to use a fine word, will more and more become a reflection of the profile of contemporary Swedish society. This is very logical. We are trying to assemble all friends of China, and the only ones we want to keep at bay are those openly hostile to China. But what kind of people are they?

Those striving for foreign powers to take back their former positions in Shanghai or Tientsin are so few in Sweden that I have not met a single one for several years. The handful of people in Sweden who openly do Moscow's errands is so small that it cannot even be calculated in percentages, but amounts to one or two per thousand. The inveterate and open enemies of China are insignificantly few in number.

For different reasons and in different ways, a larger group

opposes Swedish-Chinese friendship. Some of them are really enemies of China; others are perhaps only ignorant. This will be seen as time goes by. For when it comes to attitudes toward China, what is missing in Sweden is knowledge. There, we have a great task.

In our work for friendship and understanding and increased mutual exchange between Sweden and China, we can assume that the majority in the country, say ninety-seven to ninety-eight percent, are friends of China, pronouncedly or in part consciously, or else potential friends of China. It is clear that we who harbor a consciously friendly feeling toward China must work in such a way as not to repel all the thousands upon thousands of potential friends of China but, on the contrary, endeavor to make them genuine friends of China. From that it follows that the more we develop, the more distinctly we will correspond to the profile of Swedish society

But saying this is not enough. This truth about our work would remain a half-truth if we did not at the same time say that there is actually a great and underlying value-judgment behind our work, one which is common to us all and which does not merely concern the relationship between Sweden and China.

When this organization was founded twenty-five years ago, its task was to work for increased understanding and mutual exchange between Sweden and China. This meant taking a stand on the Chinese people's great victory. The Chinese people had stood up. It was a world historic event. We took a stand for friendship and mutual exchange between equal countries having equal rights, on the basis of mutual respect between the peoples.

Mutual respect and equality between nations concerns more than just the relations between Sweden and China. Thus friendship work implies taking a stand in general for non-hegemonic international relations. This stand cannot be combined with racism, cultural chauvinism or ideas of world domination or hegemony.

Friendship work thus actually means participating in work

for the new world of equality and mutual respect that is now taking shape after centuries of colonialism and whose aspirations are for world domination. Friendship work likewise really means the insight that we have mutual interests in this sense.

Our own work and our cooperation with our Chinese friends is also marked by this mutual respect. China is a large country and Sweden is a small country. But we are equals. It is not as if China were a leading country in relation to Sweden or other countries and we were satellite countries. Historical development does not follow like beads on a string. In different countries, the pace and result of social, political, technical and economic development can differ at different moments, but independent countries are equals.

This has been the clear basis of our work. It has been so self-evident, it has often remained unsaid. I bring this issue up because it is of special significance, just as we now move on from federation to popular movement, and our responsibility grows.

When we started, the new China was quite unknown in Sweden. Much can be said about this. At the same time, our main task was information. This task is still very important. For many people, it is ignorance which is an obstacle to friendship with China.

During certain periods, China has been exposed to great campaigns of lies, which have been ultimately directed by the Kremlin in recent years. It has been our task then to expose these campaigns by providing factual information about China and Chinese standpoints. We have not done this in China's interest, but in our own. It is the Swedish people who will suffer most if the fabricators of lies in the Kremlin and on Taiwan are successful in their campaigns. This task still remains important.

But as we have grown and as the exchange between Sweden and China has increased, our responsibility for this exchange has also increased. It is not as if our task is only to spread information about China in Sweden. We are not a Chinese society in Sweden, our task is to work for real friendship. This friendship can only be based on reciprocity, mutual respect, mutual understanding and mutual exchange. Friendship is mutual, a giving and receiving, an exchange. There is much to be done. The fact that the Federation can now receive a delegation from China to this country as our guests is a great success. More delegations will be received. We must work to increase the number of Chinese visits to Sweden on all levels. We must strive for them to get to know the realities of Sweden, get to know our problems as well as our successes.

Let me give you three typical examples of delegations we should invite. I would like us to invite a delegation of ethnologists and museum people from China to acquaint them with our experience. In this field, we have every reason to be proud. The lifework of Hazelius is an important legacy.* Skansen and the Northern Ethnographical Museum and what they represent are of a high international standard.

We should invite a delegation to study good and bad results of Swedish urban planning and traffic planning in densely built-up areas during the last thirty years. In this field we have made tremendous mistakes but also learned valuable lessons, and both ought to be explained. We should discuss, talk and listen to different points of view.

We should invite a delegation to study how such a thing as the environmental disaster at Techomatorp, where a whole township perished, could take place. We ought to show how our safety measures have failed there in the community.

These are examples. There are many others. But we should demand of the Swedish Government increased financial support for inviting Chinese study groups as well as an arrangement of the programs so that they show our Swedish experience from every angle.

* Dr. Arthur Hazelius (1833-1901), linguist, ethnographer and historian, pioneered in establishing the popular history of the Swedish people. He also founded the first open air museum for popular culture in the world, Skansen in Stockholm, and the museum for the history of the Swedish people, the Nordic Ethnographical Museum, also in Stockholm.

The great Chinese Archeological Exhibition in Stockholm
was a success. It deepened friendship and understanding.
Now the great Swedish Archeological Exhibition will go to
Peking. We are a small country and have a history different
from that of China. But I venture to say that this exhibition
will nevertheless be an exhibition on the same high international level. This reciprocity in cultural exchange is enhancing
the friendship between our two nations.

In the Swedish National Museum, the great Lu Hsun
exhibition will open next year. It will mean a great deal, not
only to the understanding of China but also to Swedish
culture. It is likely to be of the same importance to the
development of Swedish art as the great Mexican exhibition
was once in Sweden a generation ago. One's own culture
thrives on exchange between equals.

As we bring Lu Hsun to our country, I hope it will be
possible for our Chinese friends to become acquainted with
what we are most proud of in our cultural tradition, August
Strindberg and Ivar Lo-Johansson, and great Swedish artists
like Amein, Sven Erixon and Sven Ljungberg, to mention only a few names. For we too have much that we want
to make known and much that may meet with sympathy and
interest among the Chinese people.

The Tibetan troupe of folk artists that is coming to Sweden
next year is, in other words, not just a troupe that will appear
on the stage; it is an expression of how the mutual cultural
exchange is increasing and how, through this exchange, we in
Sweden are developing our own culture. Friendship lives and
deepens by the reciprocity of exchange. The people of Sweden
and the people of China are equals. They receive from each
other and they give to each other.

Now that the Swedish-Chinese Friendship Federation is
developing into a popular movement, responsibility and work
will increase accordingly. We have great tasks in front of us,
and great demands will be made on us. But I am convinced that
we will be successful. Work for friendship between Sweden
and China for mutual exchange is work in the interest of the

Swedish people. For there are no conflicting and hostile interests between the people of Sweden and the people of China. We are equals.

Long live friendship between our two peoples!

Loudspeaker trucks prepare to spread news of "gang of four's" defeat.

Townspeople assemble for victory march.

Men and women of Tsingtao's militia demonstrate against the gang.

Firecrackers add festive air to local demonstration celebrating the gang's fall.

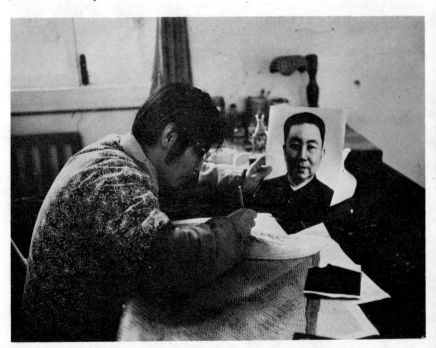

Young artist draws a picture of the new chairman, Hua Kuo-feng.

China
On the Eve of a
New Millenium

By the year 2,000, China will again be one of the world's most highly developed nations, as well as one of the leading countries in cultural and scientific spheres. These are the plans, and these have been the plans since the fifties. Political battles may have postponed their implementation a decade, and the planning may be off by a few years. In the long run, however, this is not so important for the direction is clear-cut. For those who have been interested in China, it has been clear for a long time that the plans will be realized. Construction has gone so far that anyone can see China is regaining her place. But I do not mean this as when the Ming Dynasty tried to regain the glory of the great Han and Tang dynasties. This time a socialist China is taking her place as one of the world's developed nations in a modern and technological world. It is truly a new China in every sense of the word.

For just less than a century, China was believed to be disintegrating. She was decadent, exploited, backward. Now that interlude is over. China is regaining her place, and the world is becoming normal.

China is not alone. It is only a question of time before the great nation of India regains her rightful place, not to mention Mexico, Nigeria, Brazil and Indonesia. Behind the daily jumble of headlines about war, hunger and revolt, political talk and conferences, catastrophes and contending interests, there stands out a huge drama: the emergence of the third world.

For this event, it makes no difference what we think or believe or shout. It is important to be able to see this through the jumble. I belong to those for whom this development is just and correct. Man's world is becoming normal. The era of imperialism, of domination and superpowers, is drawing to a close. The times are going along with our traditional hopes for a world of equals. This march will continue long after our lifetime.

This may sound ceremonious. That is the idea, for it is certain that this event is the historical characteristic of our generation. China will be modernized by the year 2,000. Nine hundred million, soon one thousand million people, almost a quarter of mankind, are now standing up and together exerting themselves to raise the country from poverty and backwardness. This is changing our world and concerns us all.

For China, it is not just a matter of taking a leap from agriculture by the hoe and sickle to one with tractors; it has to be a leap past known technology into the yet unknown. If a fourth of mankind attains the highest scientific level, it means that a quarter of the coming scientific breakthroughs will be Chinese.

Also, on another level, the developments in China concern us all. It is contended that China will not only succeed in catching up and regaining her place, becoming a leading scientifically and technologically advanced nation, but she will do it as a socialist society. We are shaping, they say, a new man and new institutions. Whether China succeeds—or does not succeed in breaking with past experiences of industrialization and construction, showing that progress apparently has not made a society of free, equal and creative people—this will be of importance to us all.

But there is also another consequence of China's development. She would cease to appear strange or odd or uncanny. She would again become a foreign country among many other foreign countries where other people live. In the sixteenth and seventeenth centuries, for literate Europeans, imperial China and Mogul India were great and interesting foreign countries with rich cultures. They first became exotic and incomprehensibly "oriental" with colonialism, exploitation and oppression. When China retakes her place, the Chinese will again become not much different than Jones, Smith and Sanchez, or Meyer, O'Hara and James.

Of course, it is not an abstract "China" which has stood up and it is not "China" which is in the midst of a new long march toward the future. Rather it is the people of China who are modernizing their country through hard work and struggle. . . .

Soon to be one thousand million people, between a fifth and a fourth of the world's population, the old state with its own cultural tradition and the product of the greatest social transformation in modern history—China is indeed all of this.

China is also the largest country of the third world, the largest developing country. As China rises up out of poverty, the world is being changed.

Whatever China is, she is not a land of blue-dressed automatons. I have never understood how that notion could be spread, had it not been that writers and photographers only visited China in winter and then only stayed in north China, where the people wear thickly-padded winter clothes. In the same way, Sweden should be called the land of red noses.

China is a country of enormous contrasts. Languages and customs vary. The northerner does not understand the southerner's language and the westerner and easterner do not eat the same food. Differences in income and personal standards are still great. The professor in Shanghai and the farmer in the loess country live, to all appearances, in two different worlds. Nevertheless, China's unity is incontestable. The revolution which is still going on is changing every village, every city, and every person's life.

China is a developing country. Not too long ago, she was believed condemned to disintegration through internal strife between local warlords, each ruling over landed areas as large as European countries. Foreign troops occupied the coastal cities. Foreign lords controlled the trade. The people sank deeper and deeper into misery. When eight million starved to death, there was hardly a line in Shanghai's newspapers, not to mention how indifferently the issue was treated in the European press. In Europe, money was collected to convert the heathen Chinese to Christianity. In the United States, prayers were said for their salvation, and war vessels were then sent to Shanghai to secure profits from the work of both the baptized and unbaptized. It so happened that there were some missionaries who took almost seriously this talk about love and tried to assuage the misery about them.

The revolution began like a trickle, it is said; it murmured in the mountains. It grew to a stream which edged up over the rocks, and it swelled and rose and pushed forward as an ever more powerful river which swept millions with it, pushed aside all dams and ran ahead. But there's more to the picture than this. It shows only the force and destruction and irresistibility.

The revolution was also a liberation to construction, cooperation and new dreams. A gray layer was stricken from daily life and the world became new, as if morning. During the first year after Liberation, the youth danced every night in the streets of Peking.

Then the work began. No deliverance from the misery of reality comes from the heavens. No condescending saviors, no gods, emperors or important leaders will come in the future as a gift to the people. No, the hundreds of millions themselves must dig their way out of poverty, and their future can only be shaped by their own joint efforts.

By and large, most have been in agreement about the direction matters should take—toward an equal and just society. But for sure, the hundreds of millions have not all been in agreement about the means of accomplishing this, and great political battles between small groups of some tens of millions have shaken the country. The many hundreds of millions had for their own sake to throw themselves into the great discussion and take hold of the helm of state.

Right now, a period of stability and order reigns; goal-oriented work for future construction is being carried out. But out of this tranquil period will erupt new battles where new millions of people raise the issue of what the character of this new and better society they are building should be. There is a time to break down and a time to build up. Just which slogans will cause new storms, no one knows today. But the direction things are going in is certainly a given.

For thirty years, the people have worked and toiled, and year after year, the new society has been built. Already most of those who are old and who lived through the real misery of the past have gone. The new reality which has been shaped seems dry and poor for the intellectual youth in Shanghai, Peking and other big cities. They envision a future of skyscrapers and air conditioners and wish themselves a new, better and more equal America. In its own way, the American dream is as popular as it was in Europe after the war. This does not signify self-effacement or infatuation with the dark seamy sides of the United States. But as in the Soviet Union during the thirties and in Western Europe in the fifties, one longs for the new technology and the new prosperity. It is easy to say that this prosperity of an American type is only materialistic. But tell this to those who live with their whole family in a single room, who share the water faucet with five other families, who have no access to the garden, who stand in bus lines early each morning, who weigh their few pennies each time before buying their ration of rice, cotton or whatever, and who have never yet had a decent vacation. It is a better America and an equal America one wants, where no one will live in poverty and slums.

This dream of America, which has been and is so strong in China, does not mean the United States should have military, political and economic hegemony in China, nor even that those who harbor dreams of America are willing to give the United States special advantages.

Each time the questions are posed, in the twenties, thirties or forties—or after Liberation when the United States chose to oppose the Chinese people, or when the U.S. participated in the Korean War, or invaded Vietnam and Cambodia—it has become clear that the great American dream is a Chinese dream. They are longing for technology and material goods, they feel a fellowship with frankness and openness, they read Mark Twain and speak about Lincoln. . . .this is precisely why they oppose the United States' attempts to dominate China economically, politically and militarily. They believe they are in agreement with most typical Americans.

Now this "they" I write of does not make up everyone. In the interior, among the poor peasants, the issue is another. There they have no American dream. Many among them find it difficult to convince themselves that they need go much further than they have come. A few decades ago, their revolution was victorious. Now they have roofs over their heads and security for their later years. Like everyone of past generations, they have to work by the sweat of their brow. The plough is good enough.

There are many contradictions and conflicts in China which are seldom revealed in the wall newspapers of Peking. And they are never discussed when one wonders which leaders in a photo stand where and who has hinted what about whom with which slogans.

This is the way things are in a developing socialist country, and this is the way things will be for a long time to come.

What is happening in China concerns us all. The Chinese people, as I have stated earlier, have carried out the most sweeping revolution of this century and are now conducting the most vast deep-going transformation and modernization of society. China is no longer *exotic;* she is a great neighbor to all of us around the world.*

*The preceding article was excerpted from a Swedish Broadcasting Corporation/Channel One press release of December 13, 1978.

Jan Myrdal was born July 9, 1927, in Stockholm, Sweden. He started working as a newspaper reporter in 1944 and produced his first book in 1953. Since that time, some fourty-four volumes of his writing—including plays, novels and historical works—have been published. Eighteen of these works have been translated into twenty different languages.

Myrdal has traveled widely in Europe and Asia and written extensively about these travels. The author is also a regular columnist for *Folket i Bild/Kulturfront,* a progressive cultural publication in Sweden. Most recently, he collaborated on a series of films for Swedish television.

China Notebook: 1975-78 is his fourth book about China to be translated into English. Myrdal has been visiting and writing about China since the early 1960s, when that country opened her doors to the first Western writers and tourists. *Report from a Chinese Village,* published in 1964, was the result of that first visit and a month's stay in the village of Liu Lin. The book was declared a "social classic" by Harrison Salisbury; "a book rich in its account of human conditions," said Edgar Snow.

In 1969, Myrdal returned to Liu Lin and his impressions of the developments there since the start of the Cultural Revolution are recorded in *China: The Revolution Continued,* published in 1971.

Gun Kessle is a well-known Swedish artist and photographer. She studied in London and at the Royal Academy in Stockholm. She is married to Jan Myrdal and has collaborated with him on several of his books. Gun Kessle has also written and illustrated a number of books of her own and is currently a board member of *Förr och Nu,* a Swedish magazine of popular culture.

TRANSLATOR'S NOTE. The Pinyin system of translating the Chinese language into English has recently been adopted by the Chinese publishing industry, as well as the U.S. State Department, the United Nations and all the major wire services. *China Notebook: 1975-78* was translated before Pinyin became widely adopted, and the book, therefore, employs the Wade-Giles system which had been in use since 1867.